Librar

Library materials mus   st
date stamped or fine   t
rate. Items can be re   er
or personal call unless required by another borrower.
For hours of opening and charges see notices
displayed in libraries.

2.10.13		
28/01/15		
1 6 FEB 2015		
1 6 AUG 2016		
2 6 MAR 2018		

915 00000006455

Exciting Food for Southern Types

PELLEGRINO ARTUSI

PENGUIN BOOKS

PENGUIN BOOKS

Published by the Penguin Group
Penguin Books Ltd, 80 Strand, London WC2R 0RL, England
Penguin Group (USA) Inc., 375 Hudson Street, New York, New York 10014, USA
Penguin Group (Canada), 90 Eglinton Avenue East, Suite 700, Toronto, Ontario,
Canada M4P 2Y3 (a division of Pearson Penguin Canada Inc.)
Penguin Ireland, 25 St Stephen's Green, Dublin 2, Ireland
(a division of Penguin Books Ltd)
Penguin Group (Australia), 250 Camberwell Road,
Camberwell, Victoria 3124, Australia
(a division of Pearson Australia Group Pty Ltd)
Penguin Books India Pvt Ltd, 11 Community Centre,
Panchsheel Park, New Delhi – 110 017, India
Penguin Group (NZ), 67 Apollo Drive, Rosedale, Auckland 0632, New Zealand
(a division of Pearson New Zealand Ltd)
Penguin Books (South Africa) (Pty) Ltd, 24 Sturdee Avenue,
Rosebank, Johannesburg 2196, South Africa

Penguin Books Ltd, Registered Offices: 80 Strand, London WC2R 0RL, England

www.penguin.com

La scienza in cucina e l'arte di mangiare bene first published in Italy 1891
This translation, *Science in the Kitchen and the Art of Eating Well*, first published in the
USA by Marsilio Publishers 1997
This extract published in Penguin Books 2011

1

LEWISHAM
LIBRARY SERVICE

Askews & Holts	28-Sep-2012
641.59457	

ISBN: 978–0–241–95110–1

www.greenpenguin.co.uk

MIX
Paper from
responsible sources
FSC® C018179

Penguin Books is committed to a sustainable
future for our business, our readers and our
planet. This book is made from paper certified
by the Forest Stewardship Council.

Contents

A Note

Cooking is a troublesome sprite. Often it may drive you to despair. Yet it also very rewarding, for when you do succeed, or overcome a difficulty in doing so, you feel the satisfaction of a great triumph.

Beware of books that deal with this art: most of them are inaccurate or incomprehensible, especially the Italian ones. The French are a little better. But from either, the very most you will glean are a few notions, useful only if you already know the art.

If you do not aspire to become a premier cook, you need not have been born with a pan on your head to become a good one. Passion, care, and precision of method will certainly suffice; then, of course, you must choose the finest ingredients as your raw materials, for these will make you shine.

The best teacher is experience, under an adept's watchful eye. Yet even lacking this, with a guide such as mine, and devotion to your labors, you should be able, I hope, to put something decent together.

If at first you do not succeed, do not despair; with good will and persistence, you shall manage to make these dishes one day, I guarantee it, and perhaps even to improve them. For I, after all, cannot presume to have reached the acme of perfection.

Yet I may discreetly assume that my dishes have been

generally well received, and that to my great fortune few people, thus far, have cursed me for stomach aches or other phenomena that decency forbids me to mention.

Finally, I should not like my interest in gastronomy to give me the reputation of a gourmand or glutton. I object to any such dishonorable imputation, for I am neither. I love the good and the beautiful wherever I find them, and hate to see anyone squander, as they say, God's bounty. Amen.

———————

From the Author to the Reader

Life has two principal functions: nourishment and the propagation of the species. Those who turn their minds to these two needs of existence, who study them and suggest practices whereby they might best be satisfied, make life less gloomy and benefit humanity. They may therefore be allowed to hope that, while humanity may not appreciate their efforts, it will at least show them generous and benevolent indulgence.

The meaning contained in these few lines, which preface the third edition of this book, was better expressed in a letter to me by the celebrated poet, Lorenzo Stecchetti. It is my pleasure to transcribe them here:

The human race survives only because man possesses the instincts of self-preservation and reproduction, and keenly feels the need to satisfy both. The satisfaction of a need is always accompanied by pleasure. The pleasure of self-preservation lies in the sense of taste, and that of reproduction in the sense of touch. If man did not find food appetizing, or experience sexual desire, the human race would quickly come to an end.

Taste and touch are therefore the senses most necessary, indeed indispensable to the life of the individual and the species. The other senses are only there to help, and one can, after all, live life blind and deaf, but not without the functional activity of the organs of taste.

How is it, then, that on the scale of the senses, the two most necessary to life and its continuance are considered the basest? Why are those things that satisfy the other senses – painting, music, etc. – called art and deemed noble, while those that satisfy the sense of taste are considered ignoble? Why is a person who enjoys gazing at a lovely painting or listening to a beautiful symphony held in higher esteem than one who enjoys eating an excellent dish? Is the equality among the senses perhaps comparable to that among humans, whereby those who work may be well off, but those who do not are even better off?

The blame, no doubt, must lie with the tyrannical sway the brain now holds over all the organs of the body. In the time of Menenius Agrippa, the stomach ruled; nowadays it no longer even serves, or, if so, serves badly. Of all those who over-work their brains, is there a single one who can boast of good digestion? They are all nerves, neuroses, and neurasthenia. The height, chest-size, strength and reproductive powers of this ingenious, rachitic breed of sages and artists, all refine-ment and glands, are in daily decline. Indeed they do not even eat, but rather overstimulate themselves and keep going by dint of coffee, alcohol and morphine. Thus are the senses that direct the brain's functions deemed nobler than those that pre-side over self-preservation – and the time has come to right this unjust verdict.

God bless the bicycle, which lets us know the joys of a hearty appetite, notwithstanding all the decadent and decayed who dream of chlorosis, consumption and boils in the name of the ideal art! Let us go out, out into the open air, into the free-flowing, healthy air! It reddens the blood and strengthens the muscles! Let us not be ashamed, therefore, to eat the best we can and return gastronomy to its rightful place. In the end, even the tyrannical brain will be the better for it, and this nerve-wracked society will finally understand that, even in art, a discussion on how to cook eel is every bit as worthy as a disquisition on the smile of Beatrice.

It is true that man does not live by bread alone; he must eat something with it. And the art of making this something as economical, savory and healthy as possible is, I insist, a true art. Let us rehabilitate the sense of taste and not be ashamed to satisfy it honestly, and as best we can, according to its own dictates.

I beg the kind Ladies and good Housewives, for whom this work of great effort and expense is intended, to study it with love, for they will derive great advantage from it. May they continue to bestow their much-desired favor on me, and I shall be a happy man.

First Courses

It used to be said that pasta was the forage of man. Today doctors advise us to eat it sparingly, lest it overly dilate the stomach and reduce our consumption of meat. Meat strengthens the body's fibers, while starches, which pastas are usually made of, create fatty tissue, which cause flabbiness. To this theory I raise no objection; but if I may be permitted, I would like to make the following suggestions. Small amounts of pasta are for anyone who, not being in his prime or in perfect health, must be treated with special care. Small amounts of pasta are also for those who tend to put on weight and would like to keep such gains in check. Finally, small portions of pasta with a light sauce should be served at banquets, if the guests are to do justice to the various dishes that follow. But aside from these cases, a good and generous helping of pasta will always be welcome at humbler dinners, so go ahead and enjoy it. Governed by this principle, I shall make a point of listing every kind of pasta and soup that experience suggests to me.

Peas with bacon (see page 54) can give flavor and charm, as we all know, to soups made with rice, pastina and malfattini. But if you have no broth, they are better used in risotto (see page 15).

1

CAPPELLETTI ALL'USO DI ROMAGNA
(*Cappelletti Romagna Style*)

They are called cappelletti (or 'little hats') because of their hat-like shape. This is the easiest way to make them so that they are less heavy on the stomach.

180 grams (about 6⅓ ounces) of ricotta, or half ricotta and half 'raviggiolo' (a soft cheese made from goat or sheep milk)

½ capon breast cooked in butter, seasoned with salt and pepper and finely chopped with a 'mezzaluna'

30 grams (about 1 ounce) of grated Parmesan cheese

1 whole egg

1 egg yolk

a dash of nutmeg, a few spices, some lemon zest (if desired), and a pinch of salt

Mix all the ingredients and then taste, checking for seasonings and flavor. If you do not have a breast of capon, use 100 grams (about 3½ ounces) of lean pork loin instead, cooked and seasoned as above.

If the ricotta or raviggiolo is too soft, leave out an egg white, or if the mixture comes out too firm, add another yolk. Enclose this stuffing in a soft dough made with flour and eggs only, using some of the leftover whites. Roll out the dough in a thin sheet and then cut it into disks.

Place the stuffing in the center of the disk and fold, so as to form half-moon shapes. Then take the two ends, press them together and you will have a 'cappelletto.'

If the dough dries out as you are working with it, then

dip a finger in water and wet the disks along the edges. For best results, this pasta calls for a broth made with capon, that silly animal that every year out of the goodness of its heart offers itself to be sacrificed to mankind during the solemnities of Christmas. Cook the cappelletti in the capon broth, as they do in Romagna, where, on Christmas day, you will find braggarts claiming to have eaten a hundred of them. This can also suffice to kill you, however, as happened to a friend of mine. For a moderate eater, a couple of dozen cappelletti will be quite enough.

Apropos of this pasta, I will tell you a little story, which, though it may be of little importance, may yet give pause to reflect.

You should know that the gentlemen of Romagna are not in the least interested in racking their brains over some tome, perhaps because from infancy children are accustomed to seeing their parents doing anything but turning the pages of books. Another factor may be that, being in a place where one can lead a happy and pleasurable life with little, the Romagnoli do not believe much instruction in life is necessary. For this reason, after they finish grammar school, a good ninety per cent of them takes up a life of leisure, and then no matter how hard you prod or pull, they will not budge. This was the situation a husband and wife living in a village of lower Romagna found themselves in with their teenage son Carlino. The father, however, believed in progress and, though he had the means to leave his son well provided for, would have liked the boy to become a lawyer, or possibly even a member of Parliament, since it is but a short step from one to the other. After many conversations, deliberations, and squabbles within the family over the great separation, the decision was made to send Carlino to continue his studies in a big city. Ferrara was chosen, being the nearest. Carlino's father accompanied him there, but did so with a heavy heart, having had to tear him from the arms of his loving mother, who had drenched him with tears.

Less than a week had passed. The parents were sitting down at table for a dish of cappelletti. After a long silence and several sighs, the mother exclaimed:

'Oh, if only Carlino were here! He so loves cappelletti!' No sooner were these words spoken than they heard a knock at the front door, and into the room sprang a cheerful Carlino.

'Oh, you are back!' exclaimed the father. 'What happened?'

'What happened,' replied Carlino, 'is that wasting away over books is not for me. I would rather be drawn and quartered than return to that jail.' Overjoyed, the mother ran to embrace her son, and turned to her husband.

'Let him do as he wishes,' she said. 'Better a healthy fool than a sickly scholar. He will be busy enough looking after his interests here.' Indeed, from that moment on, Carlino's interests revolved around a rifle, a hunting dog, a frisky horse hitched to a fine little racing gig, and continual assaults on the young country girls.

PANATA (*Bread Soup*)

The people of Romagna solemnly celebrate Easter with this soup and call it 'tridura,' a word whose meaning has been lost in the Tuscan dialect, but which was in use in the early 14th century. We know this because the word appears in an ancient manuscript, which mentions a ceremonial gift to the friars of Settimo at Cafaggiolo (Florence) which involved sending every year to the monastery a newly made wooden bowl full of tridura and covered by sticks that supported ten pounds of pork decked with laurel. Everything in the world grows old and changes, even languages and words, but not the ingredients of which dishes are made. For this soup, they are:

130 grams (about 4½ ounces) of day-old bread, grated, not crushed
4 eggs
50 grams (about 1⅔ ounces) of grated Parmesan cheese
a dash of nutmeg
a pinch of salt

Place the ingredients in a large saucepan and mix them together, but do not let the mixture thicken too much. However, if the mixture is too loose, add more bread crumbs. Dilute with hot but not boiling broth, setting some aside to add later. Cook with embers around the pot, but with little or no heat directly under it. When it begins to boil, try to gather it gently with a wooden spoon in the center of the saucepan by pushing it inwards from the sides of the pan, but without breaking it apart. When it has thickened and set, pour it into the soup tureen and send it to the table. These amounts are enough for six people.

If the panata has turned out well, you will see it gathered in small bunches, with the clear broth around it. If you like it with herbs and peas, cook these separately, and stir them into the mixture before you pour broth over it.

MINESTRA DI DUE COLORI
(*Two-Color Soup*)

This is a light and delicate soup which in Tuscany is most likely to be appreciated by the ladies. However, it should not be served in Romagna, that homeland of tagliatelle, where softness to the bite is not to the locals' taste. Even less would they appreciate the pasty texture of tapioca, the very sight of which would, with few exceptions, turn their stomachs.

180 grams (about 6⅓ ounces) of flour
60 grams (about 2 ounces) of butter
40 grams (about 1⅓ ounces) of Parmesan cheese
4 deciliters (about 1⅔ cups) of milk
2 whole eggs
2 egg yolks
salt to taste
a handful of spinach
a dash of nutmeg

Boil the spinach, squeeze it dry and pass it through a sieve. Heat the butter and when it has melted, add the flour, stirring well. Then add the milk, a little at a time. Salt it and, while it is cooking, work the mixture with a wooden spoon, turning it into a smooth paste.

Remove it from the heat, and when it is lukewarm add the eggs, grated Parmesan and nutmeg. Then divide the mixture into two equal parts. Use one part to blend in just enough spinach to make the mixture turn green.

Place the mixture in a pastry-tube using the attachment that has rather wide round holes. Squeeze the dough into boiling broth. This procedure must be repeated twice, once with the yellow mixture and once with the green one.

These amounts serve eight to ten people.

MALFATTINI
(*Easy Egg Noodle Soup*)

In those parts of the country where homemade egg pasta is eaten almost daily, every housemaid has mastered the art of making it, and especially this dish, which is the essence of simplicity. Thus I speak about it not for them, but for the inhabitants of those provinces who know of no other soups than those made with bread, rice or store-bought pasta.

The most simple malfattini are made with flour. Fold the eggs into the flour and knead the mixture on the pastry board until you obtain a firm loaf. Cut this into large slices a half finger thick, and leave them a while to dry in the air. Then chop them with the mezzaluna into tiny bits about half the size of a grain of rice. You can achieve consistency of size by passing them through a strainer, or by grating them from the whole loaf. But do not do as those who leave them large as sparrow's beaks, for this will make them difficult to digest. Indeed, for even easier digestion, rather than with flour, you can make them with bread crumbs, either plain or with a pinch of grated Parmesan cheese and a dash of spices.

However you make them, you can serve them with peas with bacon (see page 54) when peas are in season, or use finely diced beet, or both. *A propos* of beet, I have noticed that in Florence, where they make a great use of aromatic herbs in cooking, dill is unknown. Mixed with beet, as is done in other towns, dill graces the palate. Indeed, I have tried to introduce this fragrant herb to Florence, but with little success. Perhaps this is because in that city beets are sold in bunches, whereas in Romagna they are carried loose to the market or already mixed with dill.

MINESTRONE
(*Mixed Vegetable and Rice Soup*)

Minestrone brings back memories of a year marked by collective anxiety and a singular personal experience.

In the year of Our Lord 1855, I found myself at Livorno during the bathing season. Cholera was then making its way through several provinces of Italy, gripping everyone with the fear of a major epidemic, which, in fact, was not long in coming. One Saturday evening I entered a trattoria, and asked: 'What's today's soup?'

'Minestrone,' was the answer.

'Fine, bring the minestrone,' I replied. I ate, took a stroll, and then went to bed. I had taken lodgings in the Piazza del Voltone, in a whitewashed new villa run by a certain Mr. Domenici. That night, I felt the onset of a frightening disturbance in my body that had me running regularly back and forth to the rest rooms – which in Italy should rather be called an *unrest* room. 'Damned minestrone! You will never fool me again,' I cried out, raging against something which was perhaps quite innocent.

Morning came, and feeling myself totally drained, I caught the first train and escaped to Florence, where I immediately felt much better. Monday the sad news reached me that cholera had broken out in Livorno, and the first to be struck dead was none other than Domenici himself.

And to think I had blamed the minestrone!

After three attempts, improving upon the dish each time, this is how I like to make it. Feel free to modify it to suit the tastes of your part of the world, and the vegetables locally available.

Start by making the usual meat broth, and cooking in it a handful of shelled fresh beans. If the beans are dry, then simmer them in water until they soften. Then cut some Savoy cabbage, spinach and a little chard into thin slices, and soak them in cold water. Then, to get the water out of the vegetables, place them on the fire in a dry saucepan. Drain the contents well, pressing them firmly with a wooden spoon to get rid of excess water. For a minestrone that serves four to five people, finely chop 40 grams (about 1⅓ ounces) of fatty prosciutto, a clove of garlic, and a sprig of parsley, and sauté them together. Add this to the saucepan, along with some celery and carrots, one potato, one zucchini, and very little onion, all cut into short, thin slices. Add the beans, and if you wish, some pork rind (as some people like to do), and a bit of tomato sauce (see page 21) or tomato paste. Season with salt and pepper and cook in the broth. As a last ingredient add enough rice to absorb most of the liquid, and before removing the minestrone from the fire throw in a good pinch of Parmesan cheese.

I should warn you that this is not a soup for weak stomachs.

ZUPPA ALLA STEFANI
(*Stefani Soup*)

The distinguished poet Olindo Guerrini, librarian of the University of Bologna, has a taste for learning so developed that he enjoys digging up the bones of the culinary paladins of old, and drawing astonishing inferences from them that make modern cooks laugh out loud. He was good enough to favor me with the following recipe, taken from a little book, *The Art of Cooking Well*, by Signor Bartolomeo Stefani of Bologna, who was the cook of His Serene Highness the Duke of Mantua in the mid-1600s. At that time, much use and abuse was made of all manner of seasonings and spices, and sugar and cinnamon were used in broth, as well as in making boiled or roasted meat. Omitting some of his instructions for this soup, I shall limit myself, aromatically speaking, to a bit of parsley and basil. And if the ancient Bolognese cook, meeting me in the afterworld, scolds me for it, I shall defend myself by explaining that tastes have changed for the better. As with all things, however, we go from one extreme to the other, and we are now beginning to exaggerate in the opposite direction, going as far as to exclude herbs and spices from dishes that require them. And I shall tell him as well of the ladies who, at my table, have made gruesome faces when confronted with a bit of nutmeg. Here is the recipe for the soup (serves six):

120 grams (about 4¼ ounces) of veal or lamb brains
    (or brains of a similar animal)
3 chicken livers
3 eggs
1 sprig of basil and 1 of parsley, chopped
the juice of ¼ lemon

Scald the brain so as to be able to skin it, and then sauté with the chicken livers in butter. Finish cooking them in brown stock, adding salt and pepper for seasoning.

Put the eggs in a pot and beat them with the basil and parsley, as well as the lemon juice and a bit of salt and pepper. Add cold broth a little at a time, to dilute the mixture. Then dice the brain and the livers and add to the pot. Put this on a low flame to thicken, stirring constantly with a wooden spoon. Take care not to bring it to a boil. After it has thickened, pour into a soup tureen over some diced bread sautéed in butter or oil and sprinkled with a handful of grated Parmesan cheese.

This is a delicate, substantial soup. However, if you, like me, are not particularly fond of foods with such a soft texture, then you may want to substitute sweetbreads for brains. And this reminds me to mention – and I know whereof I speak – that in some regions where, because of the climate, one must be careful about what one eats, the inhabitants have so enfeebled their stomachs by eating light and preferably soft, liquid dishes, that they can no longer withstand food of any weight.

ZUPPA ALLA CERTOSINA
(*Soup Carthusian Style*)

With 500 grams (about 1 pound) of fillets from a variety of fish you should be able to make enough soup for four to five people.

Finely chop ¼ of an onion, some parsley and celery. Put on the fire in a pan with oil and, when it has browned, add the fish, which you will keep moist with water, tomato sauce (see page 21) or tomato paste. Season with salt and pepper. Allow it to cook well and then add the water for the soup – 1 liter (about 1 quart) of water in total should suffice for this recipe. Pass the mixture through a sieve, pressing well against the mesh. Then put it back on the fire and bring it to a boil again. Break three eggs in a tureen and mix them with three spoonfuls of Parmesan cheese. Pour in the broth slowly, and before serving toss in small cubes of bread which you have toasted or fried in the condiment you prefer: butter, oil, or lard. If you like to see the eggs and Parmesan cheese making little lumps in the soup, you can beat them separately and pour them in the pot when the broth is boiling.

It is said that the Granduke of Tuscany first tasted this soup in a convent of friars and, having found it excellent, sent his cook there to learn how to make it. But no matter how hard he tried, the excellent cook could not make the soup as well as the friars, who did not want to tell the Granduke that the soup was made with broth of capon rather than water!

TAGLIATELLE ALL'USO DI ROMAGNA
(*Tagliatelle Romagna Style*)

'Bills should be short and tagliatelle long,' the people of Bologna say, and they are right, because long bills terrify poor husbands and short tagliatelle look like leftovers, attesting to the incompetence of their maker. For this reason I do not approve of the widespread custom adopted simply to satisfy the palate of foreigners of chopping capellini, taglierini and similar types of pasta into the minutest bits and serving them in broth. Since they are unique to Italy, they ought to preserve their original characteristics.

Prepare the pasta dough and cut it. Boil for a short while, drain well, put in a saucepan and heat for a moment to help it absorb the sauce, which is the one for country-style spaghetti (see page 16). Also add enough butter to season the amount of pasta you are making. Toss gently, then send to the table.

To my way of thinking, this is a very tasty dish, but to digest it well, you need air like the kind that you can breathe in Romagna.

I remember traveling once with some Florentines (a toothless old codger, a middle-aged man and a young lawyer) who were on their way to claim an inheritance in Modigliana. We stopped at an inn, and you can well imagine the sort of place it was in that part of the country, this being forty or more years ago. The innkeeper gave us only tagliatelle as the pasta course and cured pork neck as an appetizer, and while this was very tough and displeasing to the taste, the effort the old fellow made to gnaw it was a sight to behold. Such was the appetite he and the other two possessed, that they found this and everything else to be very good, indeed delicious; I even heard them exclaim several times: 'Oh, if only we could take this air with us to Florence!'

Speaking of that fair city, let me tell you about a certain Count from Romagna who was living in Florence when 'francesconi' were still in circulation. This gentleman, a fine match for Goldoni's *Marquis of Forlimpopoli*, had plenty of arrogance, only a few pennies to his name, and a cast-iron stomach. In those days you could live inexpensively in Florence, which was famous for its low prices in comparison to other capital cities. There were many small restaurants that offered a *prix-fixe* meal of pasta, three main courses to choose from, fruit or pastry, bread and wine for a single Tuscan lira. The servings, though small, satisfied everyone who was not as hungry as a wolf. Even the nobility frequented these restaurants, although the Count in question did not deign to do so. What trick do you suppose he had found to maintain such a façade while spending little? On alternate days he would go to the buffet table at one of the best hotels, where for half a francescone (2.80 lire), the fare offered was most sumptuous. Gobbling up everything in sight, he would stuff his stomach enough to last him two days. Then he would go home to diet, on the off day, on bread, cheese and cold cuts. Now you have his example and the recipe.

RISOTTO COI PISELLI
(*Rice with Peas*)

Rice! Behold the fattening food that the Turks feed to their women, so that they will develop, as a celebrated and well-known professor would say, sumptuous adipose cushions.

500 grams (about 1 pound) of rice
100 grams (about 3½ ounces) of butter
Parmesan cheese, as needed
1 medium-sized onion

Rice, as I have indicated earlier, should not be washed; it is enough to clean it and rub it in a kitchen towel.

Mince the onion very finely with a mezzaluna and put it on the fire with half the butter. When it has turned golden brown, add the rice, stirring constantly with a large spoon until it has absorbed all the butter. Then start adding hot water ladleful at a time. Make sure the rice does not boil too fast, otherwise it will remain hard in the center while becoming too soft on the outside. Salt and cook until dry, then add the rest of the butter. Before removing from the fire, stir in a suitable amount of peas with bacon (see page 54), and flavor with a good handful of Parmesan cheese.

This recipe serves five people.

SPAGHETTI ALLA RUSTICA
(*Country-Style Spaghetti*)

The ancient Romans left the consumption of garlic to the lower classes, while Alfonso King of Castile hated it so much he would punish anyone who appeared in his court with even a hint of it on his breath. The ancient Egyptians were much wiser – they worshipped garlic as a divinity, perhaps because they had experienced its medicinal properties. Indeed, it is claimed that garlic provides some benefit to those suffering from hysteria, promotes the secretion of urine, strengthens the stomach, aids digestion and, being also a vermifuge, protects the organism against epidemic and pestilential diseases. When sautéing it, however, you must be careful not to cook it too much, as then it acquires an unpleasant taste. There are many people who, ignorant of the ways of food preparation, have a horror of garlic merely because they can smell it on the breath of those who have eaten it raw or poorly cooked. As a result, they absolutely ban this plebeian condiment from their kitchens. This fixation, however, deprives them of healthy and tasty dishes, such as the one I present below, which has often comforted my stomach when upset.

> Finely chop two garlic cloves and a few sprigs of parsley, as well as some basil leaves, if you like the taste. Sauté in a good measure of olive oil. As soon as the garlic starts to turn golden brown, toss in 6 or 7 chopped tomatoes, seasoning with salt and pepper. When everything is well cooked, purée the sauce, which will serve

four to five people. Pour the sauce over spaghetti or vermicelli, adding grated Parmesan cheese. Remember to cook the pasta only for a short time in plenty of water. Send to the table immediately, so that the pasta does not have time to absorb all the moisture, and thus remains of the right consistency.

Tagliatelle are also delicious when served in this sauce.

Appetizers

Appetizers or antipasti are, properly speaking, those delicious trifles that are made to be eaten either after the pasta course, as is practiced in Tuscany, which seems preferable to me, or before, as is done elsewhere in Italy. Oysters, cured meats such as prosciutto, salami, mortadella, and tongue, or seafood such as anchovies, sardines, caviar, 'mosciame' (which is the salted back of the tuna fish), etc., may be served as appetizers, either alone or with butter. In addition, the fried breads I describe below make excellent appetizers.

CROSTINI DI CAPPERI
(Canapés with Capers)

50 grams (about 1⅔ ounces) of pickled capers
50 grams (about 1⅔ ounces) of powdered sugar
30 grams (about 1 ounce) of raisins
20 grams (about ⅔ of an ounce) of pine nuts
20 grams (about ⅔ of an ounce) of untrimmed prosciutto
20 grams (about ⅔ of an ounce) of candied fruit

Coarsely chop the capers. Remove all the stems from the raisins and wash them well. Slice the pine nuts crosswise into three sections, finely dice the prosciutto, and chop the candied fruit into little chunks.

In a small saucepan heat a heaping teaspoon of flour and the two tablespoons of sugar. When the mixture begins to brown, pour in a half glass of water with a few drops of vinegar in it. Let it boil until smooth, then toss all the other ingredients into the saucepan and let simmer for 10 minutes. Test for flavor from time to time to make sure the sweet, strong taste is just right (I have not specified how much vinegar is needed, because not all vinegars are of equal strength). While the mixture is still hot, spread it over small slices of bread fried in good olive oil or lightly toasted.

You can serve these canapés cold even midway through dinner, to whet the appetites of your table companions. The best bread to use is the kind baked in a mold, as in England.

CROSTINI DI FEGATINI
DI POLLO
(*Canapés with Chicken Livers*)

As you know the gall bladder must be removed unbroken from a chicken liver, a procedure you can best perform in a small basin of water.

Put the chicken livers on the fire together with a battuto made with a shallot or, if you do not have any, a section of a small white onion, a small piece of fat trimmed from prosciutto, a few sprigs of parsley, celery and carrot, seasoned with a little olive oil and butter, as well as salt and pepper. Be sparing with the amounts, so that the resulting mixture will not turn out too spicy or heavy. When half done, remove the chicken livers from the saucepan and chop finely with a mezzaluna along with two or three chunks of dried mushrooms soaked in water. Put them back in the saucepan, and finish cooking, adding some broth. Before serving, however, sprinkle the mixture with a pinch of bread crumbs to bind it and add a little lemon juice.

Sauces

The best sauce you can offer your guests is a happy expression on your face and heartfelt hospitality. Brillat-Savarin used to say, 'Inviting someone is the same as taking responsibility for their happiness and well-being for as long as they stay under your roof.'

The pleasure you would like to give to the friends you have invited during these few hours is nowadays imperiled even before it starts by certain unfortunate customs that are being introduced and threaten to become widespread. I am referring to the so-called 'digestion visit,' to be made within eight days of the meal, and to the tips distributed to the domestics for the meal served. When you have to pay for dinner, it seems best to pay a restaurateur since that way you incur no obligation to anyone. And that bothersome second visit, which is made within a set period of time, like an obligatory rhyme, and does not issue unbidden from a sincere heart, is downright silly.

SUGO DI POMODORO
(Tomato Sauce)

Later I shall speak about another kind of tomato sauce that we call 'salsa,' as opposed to 'sugo.' Sugo must be simple and therefore composed only of cooked, puréed tomatoes. At the most you can add a few chunks of celery or some parsley or basil leaves, when you think these flavors will suit your needs.

SALSA DI MAGRO PER CONDIRE
LE PASTE ASCIUTTE
(Meatless Sauce for Pasta)

If I may be allowed to make a comparison between the senses of sight and taste, this sauce is like a young woman whose face is not particularly striking or attractive at first glance, but whose delicate and discreet features you might indeed find attractive upon closer observation.

500 grams (about 1 pound) of spaghetti
100 grams (about 3⅓ ounces) of fresh mushrooms
70 grams (about 2½ ounces) of butter
60 grams (about 2 ounces) of pine nuts
6 salted anchovies
7 or 8 tomatoes
¼ of a large onion
1 teaspoon of flour

Place half the butter in a saucepan on the fire and brown the pine nuts in it. Then remove them from the pan, and grind them in a mortar, adding the flour. Finely mince the onion, place it in the butter in which you sautéed the pine nuts, and, when it begins to brown, add the tomatoes, chopped up. Season with salt and pepper. When the tomatoes are done, purée them. Put the sauce back on the fire adding the fresh mushrooms, cut into thin slices no larger than pumpkin seeds, the pine nut paste diluted in a little water, and the rest of the butter. Allow to simmer for half an hour, adding water to make the sauce rather liquid. Lastly, dissolve the anchovies by heating them with a little of this sauce, but do not let them come to a boil, and then combine with everything else.

Drain the spaghetti and toss with the sauce. If you wish to improve this dish further, add some grated Parmesan cheese.

These amounts serve five people.

SALSA DI POMODORO
(*Tomato Sauce*)

There once was a priest from Romagna who stuck his nose into everything, and busy-bodied his way into families, trying to interfere in every domestic matter. Still, he was an honest fellow, and since more good than ill came of his zeal, people let him carry on in his usual style. But popular wit dubbed him Don Pomodoro (Father Tomato), since tomatoes are also ubiquitous. And therefore it is very helpful to know how to make a good tomato sauce.

Prepare a battuto with a quarter of an onion, a clove of garlic, a finger-length stalk of celery, a few basil leaves and a sufficient amount of parsley. Season with a little olive oil, salt and pepper. Mash 7 or 8 tomatoes and put everything on the fire, stirring occasionally. Once you see the sauce thickening to the consistency of a runny cream, pass it through a sieve and it is ready to use.

This sauce lends itself to innumerable uses, as I shall indicate in due course. It is good with boiled meat, and excellent when served with cheese and butter on pasta, as well as when used to make risotto.

SALSA DEL PAPA (*Pope Sauce*)

Do not get the idea that this sauce takes its name from the Pope in the Vatican, and is therefore some sort of extravagant delight. All the same it is rather good on fried cutlets.

Take a small handful of capers, squeezing out the brine, and an equal amount of sweetened olives, from which you have removed the pits. Mince both with a mezzaluna. Finely chop a bit of onion and put it on the fire with some butter. When the onion begins to brown, moisten it a little at a time with water until it dissolves. Then add the mixture of capers and olives and allow to simmer for a while, eventually adding a droplet of vinegar, a pinch of flour and a little more butter. Finally, add a minced anchovy, and send to the table without letting the sauce simmer any further.

SALSA TARTUFATA (*Truffle Sauce*)

Prepare a well-minced battuto with a small, nut-size chunk of onion, a half clove of garlic and a little parsley. Put on the fire with 20 grams (about ⅔ of an ounce) of butter and, when the onion begins to brown, add two fingers of Marsala or white wine in which you have first dissolved a heaping teaspoon of flour. Season the sauce with a pinch of salt, pepper and the usual spices, stirring constantly with a wooden spoon.

When the flour has thickened the sauce, add a little broth and then add some truffle shavings. Allow to stand for a moment longer on the fire, and serve as a garnish for fried cutlets of milk-fed veal, steaks or roasted meats.

I warn you that wine as a condiment is hard on some stomachs.

Fried Foods

CRESCENTE (*Half Moons*)

What a strange language they speak in learned Bologna! They call carpets rags; wine flasks gourds; sweetbreads milks. They say 'sigàre' for 'piangere' (to weep), and they call an unsavory, ugly, annoying woman, who would normally be termed a 'calia' or a 'scamonea' a 'sagoma' (Italian for silhouette and, figuratively speaking, a funny person). In their restaurants you find 'trefoils' (instead of truffles), Florentine style 'chops' (instead of 'steaks'), and other similar expressions that would drive anybody mad. It was there that, I think, the term 'batteries' was devised to describe harness races, and where 'zone' is used to mean a tram route. When I first heard the Bolognese mention a crescent, I thought they were talking about the moon. Instead they were discussing the schiacciata or focaccia, the ordinary fried dough cake that everybody recognizes and all know how to make. The only difference is that the Bolognese, to make theirs more tender and digestible, add a little lard when mixing the flour with cool water and salt.

It seems the schiacciata will puff up better if you drop it in a skillet where the fat is sizzling, but which you have removed from the fire.

The Bolognese are, in any case, an active, industrious,

friendly and hospitable people, and one speaks freely with the men, as well as the women, because their candid manner of conversation is quite engaging. If I had to judge in these matters, I would hold that this is the hallmark of a people's general civility and good manners, and not at all like what one encounters in certain other cities whose inhabitants are of an altogether different character.

In one of his tales, Boccaccio, speaking of the Bolognese, exclaims: 'Ah, how singularly sweet is the blood of Bologna! How admirably you rise to the occasion in such moments as these (moments of love)! Sighs and tears were never to your liking: entreaties have always moved you, and you were ever susceptible to a lover's yearnings. If only I could find words with which to commend you as you deserve, I should never grow tired of singing your praises!'

FRITTO ALLA GARISENDA
(*Garisenda Fry*)

You ladies who take pleasure in fine cuisine, do not consign this dish to oblivion, for it will delight your husbands, and due to the ingredients it contains, may well move them to reward you.

Take some stale bread, not too spongy, remove the crust and cut into diamond shapes or squares about 4 centimeters (about 1½ inches) on each side. On each piece place a slice of untrimmed prosciutto, then little shavings of truffle, and over them a slice of Gruyère cheese. Cover the filling with a second slice of bread and press tightly together so that they remain joined. Remember to slice everything very fine so that the pieces do not turn out inelegantly large.

Now that you have prepared the morsels, lightly soak them in cold milk, and when that has been absorbed, dip each piece in beaten egg and then roll in bread crumbs. Repeat the procedure twice so that even the edges remain covered and tightly closed.

Fry in lard or olive oil and serve alone or with another fried food.

Entrements

GNOCCHI ALLA ROMANA
(Roman-Style Dumplings)

These gnocchi, for which I have modified the amounts as follows, I hope will please you as much as they have delighted those for whom I have prepared them. Should that happen, toast to my health if I am still alive or say a *requiescat* in my name, if I have gone on to feed the cabbages.

150 grams (about 5¼ ounces) of flour
50 grams (about 1⅔ ounces) of butter
40 grams (about 1⅓ ounces) of Gruyère cheese
20 grams (about ⅔ of an ounce) of grated Parmesan cheese
½ a liter (about ½ a quart) of milk
2 eggs

It is commonly said that one should not sit down to table in lesser number than the Graces or in greater number than the Muses. If you are approaching the number of the Muses, double the amounts.

In a saucepan, mix the flour and the eggs, then pour the milk in a little at a time. Add the Gruyère cheese chopped into little pieces, and put the mixture on the fire, stirring constantly. When the flour makes it thicken, salt and add half the butter. Allow to cool, and then, in the same way as you would prepare cornmeal gnocchi, place the mixture in little tidbits onto an ovenproof platter. Season them with the rest of the butter, cut into little pats, and with the Parmesan cheese, but do not cover the top layer, because Parmesan on top turns bitter when heated. Brown under an iron lid or in a Dutch oven, and serve hot.

MACCHERONI COL PANGRATTATO
(*Macaroni with Bread Crumbs*)

If it is true, as Alexandre Dumas *père* remarks, that the English live on roast beef and pudding; the Dutch on oven-cooked meat, potatoes and cheese; the Germans on sauerkraut and bacon; the Spanish on chickpeas, chocolate and rancid bacon; and the Italians on macaroni, do not be too surprised if I keep coming back to this topic, since I have, after all, always loved this pasta. Indeed, I once very nearly acquired the distinguished name of Macaroni-Eater, and I will tell you why.

One day in 1850, I found myself in the 'Tre Re' (Three Kings) restaurant in Bologna in the company of several students and Felice Orsini, who was a friend of one of them. It was the season for politics and conspiracy in Romagna, and Orsini, who seemed practically born for that purpose, spoke enthusiastically about these subjects. In his passion he tirelessly strove to show us that an uprising was imminent, that he and another leader he mentioned would lead it, overrunning Bologna with an armed band of followers. Listening to him so imprudently discuss in a public place such dangerous subjects and an enterprise that seemed to me utter madness, I remained indifferent to his harangues and calmly continued to eat the plate of macaroni set before me. My demeanor stung Orsini's *amour propre*, and thereafter, having felt humiliated at the time, whenever he remembered me he would ask his friends, 'How's the Macaroni-Eater doing?'

In my mind's eye I still see that congenial young man, of middling height, lean build, pale round face, refined features, the blackest eyes, crinkly locks, who lisped slightly when he spoke. Another time, many years later, I ran into him in a coffeehouse at Medola just as he was bristling with anger against someone who had abused his trust and offended his honor. He was asking a young fellow to follow him to Florence, to help him, he said, execute an exemplary vendetta. A series of circumstances and events, each stranger than the last, later led him to his tragic end, which we all know and deplore, but which also perhaps prodded Napoleon III to intervene in Italy. Now let's get back to our subject.

300 grams (about 10½ ounces) of long macaroni that hold up well when cooked
15 grams (about ½ an ounce) of flour
60 grams (about 2 ounces) of butter
60 grams (about 2 ounces) of Gruyère cheese
40 grams (about 1⅓ ounces) of Parmesan cheese
6 deciliters (about 2½ cups) of milk
bread crumbs, as needed

If you want to add more flavor, increase the amounts of the condiments.

Cook the macaroni halfway, salt, and drain in a colander. Put the flour on the fire in a saucepan with half the butter, stirring constantly. When the flour begins to change color, pour in the milk a little at a time and allow to boil for about 10 minutes. To this béchamel, add the macaroni and the Gruyère cheese, either grated or in little chunks. Move the saucepan to the edge of the hearth, so that the macaroni will absorb all the milk while bubbling slowly. Now add the rest of the butter and the grated Parmesan cheese. Then transfer to an ovenproof platter, fill the platter to the rim and cover with bread crumbs.

Put the macaroni prepared in this fashion into a Dutch oven or under an iron hood heated from above. When browned, serve hot as an *entremets*, or preferably, as a side dish for meat.

MIGLIACCIO DI FARINA DOLCE VOLGARMENTE CASTAGNACCIO
(*Chestnut Flour Cake, Popularly Called Castagnaccio*)

Here too, I can hardly refrain from railing against the disinclination we Italians have for commerce and industry. In some Italian provinces, chestnut flour is completely unknown and I think no one has ever even tried to introduce it. And yet for common folk, and for those unafraid of wind, it is a cheap, healthy and nutritious food.

I questioned a street vendor in Romagna on the subject. I described this chestnut cake to her, and asked why she did not try to earn a few pennies selling it. 'What can I tell you?' she replied. 'It's too sweet; nobody would eat it.' 'But those "cottarone" you are selling, aren't they sweet? Still, they are selling,' I said. 'Why don't you at least try the chestnut cake,' I added. 'At first, distribute them free to the children, give them a piece as a gift to see if they start liking the taste. And then the grown-ups are very likely to come after the children.' It was no use; I might as well have been talking to a stone wall.

'Cottarone,' for those who do not know them, are apples and pears, mostly overripe, that are stewed in the oven in a small pan with a little water in it, while the top of the pan is covered with a moist kitchen towel. But let us turn to the very simple way to make this chestnut cake.

Take 500 grams (about 1 pound) of chestnut flour, and because it easily clumps up, sift before using it to make it soft and fluffy. Then put it into a bowl and season with a small pinch of salt. This done, add 8 deciliters (about 3⅓ cups) of cool water, pouring it in a little at a time, until the mixture has the consistency of a runny porridge into which you will throw a handful of pine nuts. Some people supplement the pine nuts with chopped walnuts; others add raisins and a few rosemary leaves.

Now take a baking pan where the chestnut cake can rise to a thickness of one and half fingers. Cover the bottom with a thin layer of olive oil, pour in the chestnut porridge, and sprinkle another two tablespoons of olive oil on top. Take it to the baker to cook in the oven or bake it at home in a Dutch oven with fire above and below. Remove and serve hot.

You can also make fritters with this batter.

PIZZA A LIBRETTI
(*Accordion Cake*)

A woman wrote to me: 'I want to teach you, as I had promised myself to do, how to make a tasty and elegant fried pastry. But heaven help you if you call it flat, because it should turn out quite otherwise. Call it "accordion cake," which would be a fair description.'

Obediently carrying out the lady's orders, I tried out this accordion cake twice, and both times it turned out well. Now I will describe it to you.

Roll out a sheet of dough that is not too firm and as thin as possible by mixing together some flour, two eggs, a pinch of salt, three tablespoons of cognac or spirits, or better yet fumetto. Grease the dough with 20 grams (about ⅔ of an ounce) of melted butter and roll it up, that is fold it upon itself so that it is 10 to 11 centimeters (about 4 to 4¼ inches) wide. Make sure that the inner side is the greased side. Now cut the roll in half lengthwise and then slice crosswise at regular intervals to obtain a number of rectangles. Now press firmly with your fingers on the outer edge of each rectangle, that is, the uncut spine of the rolls. Fry in a skillet with a lot of oil, and before serving, sprinkle confectioners' sugar on top. If they have turned out well, you will see the accordions pop open and stay open.

These amounts serve four people.

Stews

POLLO ALLA MARENGO
(Chicken Marengo)

The evening of the Battle of Marengo, after the turmoil of the day, the cook to the First Consul and to the Generals was unable to find the kitchen wagons; and so he had some chickens stolen and improvised a dish that, prepared more or less as I will describe it to you, was called 'Chicken Marengo.' They say it was always a favorite of Napoleon, not so much for its intrinsic merit, but because it reminded him of that glorious victory.

Take a young chicken, remove the neck and legs and cut into large pieces at the joints. Sauté in 30 grams (about 1 ounce) of butter and one tablespoon of olive oil, seasoning with salt, pepper, and a dash of nutmeg. When the pieces have browned on both sides, skim the fat and add a level tablespoon of flour and a deciliter (about 7 fluid ounces) of wine. Add broth and cover, cooking over low heat until done. Before removing from the fire, garnish with a pinch of chopped parsley; arrange on a serving dish and squeeze half a lemon over it. The result is an appetizing dish.

FOLAGHE IN UMIDO
(*Stewed Coot*)

The coot (*Fulica atra*) could be called a fish-bird, since the Church permits it to be eaten on fasting days without infringing on Catholic precepts. The coot comes from the warm, temperate countries of Europe and North Africa. As a migratory bird, it travels by night. An inhabitant of swamps and lakes, the coot is a good swimmer, feeding on aquatic plants, insects, and small mollusks. Only two species of coot are found in Europe.

Except during the time when they lay their eggs, coots live in huge flocks, which makes for very entertaining hunting, with huge kills. Quite famous is the coot hunt called 'la tela,' which takes place several times in late autumn and winter and is conducted in small boats on Lake Massaciuccoli near Pisa, on the estate of the Marquis Ginori-Lisci. During the hunt of November 1903, in which hunters in a hundred boats from every part of Italy took part, about six thousand coots were brought down, or so the newspapers reported.

Coot meat is dark and not very flavorful, and being game it should be prepared in the following manner.

Taking, for example, four coots (as I did), skin them and singe them on the fire to remove all their down, then clean and wash them well. Thread them lengthwise on a red-hot skewer, then cut the birds into four parts, discarding the head, feet, and wing tips. Marinate for an hour in vinegar and then wash repeatedly with cool water. I did not use the livers; but I did use the gizzards, which are large and chewy like those of a chicken. Cleaned, washed and cut into four pieces, they went into the marinade.

Now, finely chop a large onion, and the appropriate amount of the usual flavorings, that is, celery, carrot, and parsley. Put this battuto on the fire with 80 grams (about 2⅔ ounces) of butter, the coots, and the gizzards. Season with salt, pepper, and a dash of spices. When the meat starts to dry out, pour in tomato sauce (see page 21) or tomato paste diluted in a generous amount of water to finish cooking and so that there will be plenty of sauce left at the end. When the birds are done, strain the sauce and add to it half a coot breast, finely minced, and another 40 grams (about 1⅓ ounces) of butter, along with some Parmesan cheese. You can use this sauce to flavor three eggs' worth of pappardelle or 500 grams (about 1 pound) of large flat noodles, which will be highly praised for their unique flavor. Serve the coots, with some of the sauce, as the main course, and they will not be sneered at. All of this should serve five or six people.

I have also heard that you can get quite a nice stock by boiling coots with two sausages inside.

PICCIONI IN UMIDO
(Stewed Squabs)

Here is a story about squabs that, as unbelievable as it may seem, is indeed true. Let it stand as proof of what I was telling you about the caprices of the stomach.

One day a lady asked a man who happened to be around to kill a couple of squabs for her. Well, he drowned them in a basin of water, right there in front of her. The lady was so shocked by the sight that from that day on she could never eat the flesh of that bird again.

> Garnish the birds with whole sage leaves, and put them in a pot or saucepan on top of some slices of untrimmed prosciutto. Season with olive oil, salt, and pepper. When they have browned, add a bit of butter and some broth, and then simmer until done. Before removing from the fire, squeeze a lemon on them and serve in their sauce over toasted bread. Salt them very little, on account of the prosciutto and the broth. During the season when verjuice is made, you can use that instead of lemon juice. As the old saying goes:

> *Quando sol est in leone,*
> *Bonum vinum cum popone,*
> *et agrestum cum pipione.*

> (When the sun is in Leo,
> Wine goes well with melon,
> And verjuice with pigeon.)

TORDI FINTI
(Mock Thrushes)

This dish is called mock thrushes because of the flavor that juniper berries and the combination of ingredients lend to it. It is a dish that many people like, and you would do well to try it.

To make six 'thrushes' you need:

300 grams (about 10½ ounces) of lean, boneless milk-fed veal
6 juniper berries

3 chicken livers
3 salted anchovies
3 tablespoons of olive oil
lardoon, as needed

These mock thrushes should look like small, stuffed cutlets; therefore cut the veal into six thin slices, flatten them out, give them a nice shape, and put the scraps aside. The scraps, along with the chicken livers, a bit of lardoon, the juniper berries, the anchovies (cleaned and boned), and a sage leaf, make up the mixture you will use to stuff the veal. So mince everything very fine and season with a little salt and pepper. After filling the veal slices with this mixture and rolling them up, wrap them in a thin slice of lardoon with half a sage leaf between the veal and the salt pork, and then tie them crosswise. I think that 60 grams (about 2 ounces) of lardoon in all should be enough.

Now that you have prepared the cutlets, put them over a high flame in a skillet or an uncovered saucepan with the three tablespoons of olive oil and season again lightly with salt and pepper. When they have browned all over, pour out the fat, but leave the burnt bits on the bottom of the pan; finish cooking, adding broth a little at a time, because when they are done the cutlets should be almost dry.

Untie and serve over six slices of lightly toasted bread, pouring over them the concentrated sauce that remains in the pan.

These mock thrushes are even good when served cold.

POLPETTONE
(*Meat Loaf*)

Dear Mr. Meat Loaf, please come forward, do not be shy. I want to introduce you to my readers.

I know that you are modest and humble, because, given your background, you feel inferior to many others. But take heart and do not doubt that with a few words in your favor you shall find someone who wants to taste you and who might even reward you with a smile.

This meat loaf is made with leftover boiled meat, and, though simple, it is an agreeable dish. Remove the fat from the meat and chop the rest with a mezzaluna. Season with an appropriate amount of salt, pepper, grated Parmesan cheese, one or two eggs, and two or three tablespoons of a mash made with crustless bread cooked in milk, broth, or simply in water, and flavored with a little butter. Mix everything together, shape into an oblong loaf, and sprinkle with flour. Then fry it in lard or oil, and you will see that soft as it was before, it will become firm and will acquire a delicate crust on the surface. Remove from the pan, and sauté on both sides in a skillet with butter. When you are about to serve it, coat it with two beaten eggs, a pinch of salt, and the juice of half a lemon. Make this sauce separately in a small saucepan, treating it as you would a cream sauce, and pour it over the meat loaf, which you have placed on a platter.

If the meat loaf is large, turn it over in the pan using a plate or a copper lid, as you would for a frittata; this ensures that you will not spoil it.

COTEGHINO FASCIATO
(*Spiced Pork Sausage or Cotechino Boiled in a Wrap*)

I will not pretend that this is an elegant dish, but rather one for the family, and as such it does the job perfectly well, and indeed you could even serve it to close friends. Speaking of close friends, Giusti says that people who are in a position to do so, should occasionally invite their close friends to get their mustaches greasy at their table. I am of the same opinion, even if the guests will probably proceed to speak ill of you, and of how they were treated.

Skin an uncooked cotechino weighing about 300 grams (about 10½ ounces). Take a large, thin cutlet of lean veal or beef weighing between 200 and 300 grams (about 7 and 10½ ounces), and pound well. Wrap the cutlet around the cotechino, tie it all up with twine and put on the fire in a saucepan with a bit of butter, some celery, carrot, and a quarter of an onion, all coarsely chopped. Salt and pepper are not necessary, because the cotechino contains plenty of these ingredients. If you plan to use the sauce on a first course of macaroni, add some slices of untrimmed prosciutto or some bacon. When the piece of meat has browned all over, pour in enough water to cover it halfway, and throw in some little pieces of dried mushrooms; simmer slowly until completely cooked. Strain the sauce, but add back the mushrooms, then use the sauce, along with cheese and butter, to season macaroni. Serve the cotechino as the main course, keeping it wrapped in the cutlet, but removing the twine, and garnishing it with a good amount of its own sauce.

It is a good idea to thicken the sauce for the pasta a bit with a pinch of flour. Put the flour in a saucepan with a bit of butter, and when it starts to brown pour in the sauce and boil for a while.

A side dish of carrots goes very well with this dish. First boil the carrots until two-thirds done and then finish cooking in the meat sauce.

Cold Dishes

LINGUA ALLA SCARLATTA
(Corned Tongue)

We call this 'alla scarlatta' (scarlet style) because it turns a nice red color. And it is a very fine dish, both in its appearance and its taste.

This talk of tongues brings to mind the following lines by Leopardi:

> *Il cor di tutte*
> *Cose alfin sente sazietà, del sonno,*
> *Della danza, del canto e dell'amore,*
> *Piacer più cari che il parlar di lingua,*
> *Ma sazietà di lingua il cor non sente.*

(Of all things the heart grows sated – of sleep, of love, of sweet song, and merry dance – things which give more pleasure than the tongue does in speech, and yet of the tongue the heart is never sated.)

It is true that the itch of loquacity is not satisfied as one ages; indeed, it grows in proportion as we grow older, as does the desire for good food, sole comfort of the aged who, however, ruled as they are by the inexorable dictates of nature, cannot abuse the comforts of the table, under penalty of grave discomforts. In old age, man consumes less; his organs become less and less active, his secretions imperfect, thus generating in the human body superfluous, harmful humors that cause rheumatism, gout, apoplectic fits, and similar offspring of Lady Pandora's box.

To return to the subject of tongue, take one from a large animal (veal or beef), and rub it all over with between 20 and 30 grams (about ⅔ and 1 ounce) of saltpeter, depending on the size of the tongue, until it is thoroughly absorbed. After 24 hours, wash the tongue several times with cold water, and while still wet rub it with a great deal of salt; then leave it for eight days. Be sure to turn it every morning in its brine, which is produced as the salt draws the water out of the tongue. Since the best way to cook it is to boil it, put the tongue on the fire in cold water, with its natural brine, a *bouquet garni*, and half an onion studded with two cloves; boil for three to four hours. Skin the tongue while it is still steaming hot, let it cool, and then send to the table. It makes an excellent, elegant cold dish if you accompany it with aspic.

Tongue can also be served hot, either by itself, or accompanied by potatoes or spinach.

Do not try this dish during the hot summer months, because the salt might not be sufficient to preserve it.

ÀRISTA (*Roast Saddle of Pork*)

In Tuscany, spit- or oven-roasted saddle of pork is called 'àrista.' It is usually eaten cold, since it is much better cold than hot. In this case, pork 'saddle' means the piece of the loin with the ribs still attached, which can weigh between 3 and 4 kilograms (between about 6 and 8 pounds).

Stud it with garlic, sprigs of rosemary, and a few cloves, but be parsimonious, because these herbs can come back to haunt you; season with salt and pepper.

Roast it on a spit – the best way – or in the oven without anything else, and use the drippings to brown potatoes or re-heat vegetables.

This is a convenient dish for families, because it keeps for a long time during the winter.

During the Council of 1430, convened in Florence to resolve some differences between the Roman and Greek Churches, this dish, which was known by another name at the time, was served up to the bishops and their entourage. When they found it to their liking, they began to cry '*arista, arista*' (good, good!), and that Greek word continues, four and a half centuries later, to denote saddle of pork cooked in this manner.

Vegetables and Legumes

When they are not misused, vegetables are a healthy part of cooking. They thin the blood, and when served with meat, they make it easier on the stomach. But the amount of vegetables used anywhere depends to a great extent on the climate of the place.

ZUCCHINI COL REGAMO
(Zucchini with Oregano)

Oregano (*Origanum vulgare*) is the fragrant seed of a small wild plant of the mint family or *Labiatae*.

Take some long zucchini – a goodly amount, since they shrink a great deal – and cut into round slices as thick as a large coin. Put a frying pan or copper skillet on the fire with a generous amount of olive oil. When the oil starts to sizzle, toss in the sliced zucchini just as they are, and cook over a high flame, stirring often. When they are half-way done, season with salt and pepper. When they look like they are beginning to brown, sprinkle a good pinch of oregano over them, and remove them immediately from the fire with a slotted spoon. They can be served by themselves or as a side dish, and they are sure to please.

Oregano is good for seasoning other foods as well, such as stewed mushrooms, fried eggs, anchovies, etc.

FAGIUOLINI E ZUCCHINI
ALLA *SAUTÉ*
(*Sautéed Green Beans and Zucchini*)

Cooked this way, these vegetables are served mainly as
a side dish. Now, so-called 'refined cooking' has reduced
and simplified the use of condiments and seasonings.
This might be healthier, and lighter on the stomach,
but flavor suffers considerably as a result, and that little
something that some people need to stimulate their
digestion is lacking. This is a case in point. If you are
using green beans, parboil them; if zucchini, keep them
raw and cut them into wedges or rounds, then sauté in
browned butter. Season with only small amounts of salt
and pepper.

If you then add a little brown stock or some tomato
sauce (see page 23), you will have gone beyond the
rules of foreign or modern cooking. But in my opinion,
they will taste better, and your stomach will feel more
satisfied. If you do not have brown stock or tomato
sauce, at least sprinkle the vegetables with Parmesan
cheese when you remove them from the fire.

FAGIUOLINI CON L'ODORE DI
VANIGLIA, O DI NEPITELLA
(*Green Beans with Vanilla or Calamint*)

Soak the green beans in cold water. If they are tender,
use them whole and raw, and when you put them in the
pot do not shake off too much of the water.

Finely chop a shallot, parsley, carrot, and celery, and sauté in oil. You can also use a pearl onion or an ordinary onion instead of a shallot. Season with salt and pepper, and when this has browned, add broth and strain, pressing hard against the mesh. Add some tomato sauce to the strained sauce, and then cook the green beans in it. Before removing the beans from the fire, season with two teaspoons of vanilla sugar. If you do not like this spice, use calamint instead.

FUNGHI MANGIERECCI
(*Edible Mushrooms*)

Because of their nitrogenous properties, mushrooms are the most nutritious of vegetables. Their unique aroma makes mushrooms delicious food, and it is a great shame that among its many varieties there are some poisonous ones, which only an expert, practiced eye can distinguish from the harmless varieties. Some guarantee can be provided when they are gathered in a place known by long experience to be free from danger.

In Florence, for example, they use a great many mushrooms that come from the woods in the surrounding mountains. If the season is rainy, they begin to appear in June; but the height of production is in September. In truth, it must be said that Florence has never been afflicted by misfortunes from these vegetables, perhaps because the two species that are almost exclusively consumed there are the bronze-colored 'porcini,' or *boletus* mushroom, and the 'ovoli' or Caesar's mushrooms. So great is the faith in their harmlessness that no precautions are taken with regard to their consumption, not even the one suggested by some people of boiling them in water acidulated with vinegar – a precaution which, for that matter, would come at the cost of their flavor.

Of the two varieties mentioned above, porcini are best fried or stewed; ovoli are best prepared like tripe, or grilled.

FUNGHI TRIPPATI
(*Mushrooms Tripe Style*)

Ovoli are best for this dish, which probably gets its name because the mushrooms are prepared like tripe. Ovoli or Caesar's mushrooms, as you know, are orange-yellow in color. The youngest ones are closed, and shaped like an egg, while the riper ones are open and flat. For this recipe, select young mushrooms, and after you have cleaned and washed them cut them into thin slices. Cook in butter and season with salt, pepper, and grated Parmesan cheese. They will turn out even better if you add some brown stock.

PETONCIANI (*Eggplant*)

The aubergine or eggplant is not a vegetable to be scorned, for it causes neither flatulence nor indigestion. It is very good in side dishes; even eaten by itself as a vegetable main dish, it is anything but unpleasant, especially the less bitter varieties grown in certain regions.

Small and medium-sized eggplants are preferable to the larger ones, which may be overripe and bitter.

Forty years ago, one hardly saw eggplant or fennel in the markets of Florence; they were considered to be vile because they were foods eaten by Jews. As in other matters of greater moment, here again the Jews show how they have always had a better nose than the Christians.

Fried eggplant can be served as an accompaniment to fried fish dishes; stewed eggplant goes with boiled meats; grilled eggplant goes with steak, milk-fed veal chops, or any roasted meat.

TORTINO DI PETONCIANI
(*Eggplant Casserole*)

Peel 7 or 8 eggplants, cut into thin round slices, and salt them to draw out some of their water. After letting them sit for a few hours, dredge them in flour and fry in oil.

Take an ovenproof platter and layer the slices of eggplant with grated Parmesan cheese and the tomato sauce from the recipe on p. 23, arranging them so that they form a nice mound. Beat an egg with a pinch of salt, one tablespoon of the same tomato sauce, one teaspoon of grated Parmesan, and two teaspoons of bread crumbs, and cover the surface of the mound with this mixture. Place the platter under the lid of a Dutch oven, with fire above, and when the egg mixture has hardened, serve. This dish can be served by itself, as an *entremets*, or accompanied by a meat dish.

The purpose of the egg covering is to give the dish a nicer appearance.

TARTUFI ALLA BOLOGNESE, CRUDI, ECC.
(*Truffles Bolognese Style, Raw, Etc.*)

The great quarrel between the Blacks and the Whites that prolonged strife in Italy after the devastating struggles between Guelphs and Ghibellines is threatening to erupt again with regard to truffles. But fear not, dear readers, for this time no blood will be shed – the present-day partisans of the black and the white are much more benevolent than the fierce adversaries of yesteryear.

I am a supporter of the whites, and in fact I openly declare and maintain that the black truffle is the worst there is. Other people do not share my opinion; they believe that the black truffle is more fragrant, while the white truffle has a subtler taste. But they are not taking into account the fact that black truffles quickly lose their aroma. The white truffles from Piedmont are universally prized, and the white truffles from Romagna, which grow in sandy soil, are very fragrant, although they taste of garlic. In any case, let us leave the great issue unresolved so that I can tell you how they cook truffles in Bologna, 'Bologna la grassa per chi vi sta, ma non per chi vi passa' (Bologna whose bounty is for those who live there, but not for those just passing through).

> After washing the truffles and cleaning them with a little brush dipped in cold water, as is usually done, the Bolognese cut them into very thin slices and arrange them on a tin-lined copper platter in alternating layers with very thin slices of Parmesan cheese; the first layer

should be of truffles. They season them with salt, pepper, and a generous amount of their best olive oil. As soon as the truffles start to sizzle, they squeeze a lemon over them and then remove them immediately from the fire. Some people add a few little pieces of butter; but if you do add butter, use only very little, otherwise the dish will turn out too heavy. Truffles are also eaten raw, very thinly sliced and seasoned with salt, pepper, and lemon juice.

They also go well with eggs. Beat the eggs and season them with salt and pepper. Put an appropriate amount of butter on the fire, and when it has melted, pour in the eggs and shortly thereafter the thinly sliced truffles, stirring until cooked.

Everyone knows about the aphrodisiacal properties of this food, so I will refrain from speaking about it, though I could tell some very amusing stories. It seems that truffles were discovered for the first time in the Périgord region of France, under Charles V.

I have preserved truffles for quite a long time, but not always successfully, in this way: sliced very thin, dried over the fire, seasoned with salt and pepper, covered with olive oil and then put on the fire just until the oil is heated through. Raw truffles are sometimes stored in rice to impart their fragrance to the rice.

CIPOLLINE AGRO-DOLCI
(Sweet-and-Sour Pearl Onions)

This dish does not require much thinking about, but only good taste, to get the amounts right. When prepared properly, it is an excellent accompaniment for boiled meats.

By pearl onions I mean the white ones that are a little larger than a walnut. Peel them, remove any superfluous parts, and scald in salted water. For about 300 grams (about 10½ ounces) of onions, put 40 grams (about 1⅓ ounces) of sugar in a saucepan on the fire without any water. When the sugar has melted, add 15 grams (about ½ an ounce) of flour. Stir constantly with a wooden spoon, and when the mixture has turned reddish-brown add ⅔ of a glass of vinegar water a little at a time. Let the liquid boil until any lumps that may have formed have dissolved. Then toss in the onions and shake the pan frequently; do not stir them with the spoon, because they will break apart. Taste before serving, because if they need more sugar or vinegar you are still in time to add some.

PISELLI COL PROSCIUTTO
(*Peas with Ham*)

Let's leave to the English the taste for eating boiled vegetables without any seasoning, or at the most with a little butter; we southern types need our food to be a little more exciting.

I have never found peas anywhere as good as the ones they serve in the restaurants of Rome, not so much on account of the excellent quality of the vegetables from that part of the country, but because in Rome they flavor peas with smoked ham. Having experimented a bit trying to discover how they prepare them, I might not have yet fully succeeded in reproducing their delicious flavor, but I am pretty close. Here is how to do it.

Cut in half lengthwise one or two spring onions (depending on the amount of peas), and put them on the fire with oil and a generous amount of untrimmed smoked ham diced into small cubes. Fry lightly until the ham shrinks, then toss in the peas, seasoning them with little or no salt and a pinch of pepper; stir, and finish cooking with broth, adding a little butter.

Serve either alone as a vegetable course, or as a side dish; but first discard all the onion.

PISELLI COLLA CARNESECCA
(*Peas with Bacon*)

Peas are also good prepared in the following way, but, unlike the preceding recipes, this one cannot be said to belong to fine cuisine.

Put on the fire some finely chopped bacon, garlic, parsley, and oil; season with a little salt and pepper, and when the garlic is golden brown, toss in the peas. When they have absorbed all the oil, finish cooking them in broth, or lacking that, in water.

If the pea pods are tender and fresh, they can be cooked in water and passed through a sieve. You thus obtain a purée which, when dissolved in broth, adds a delicate flavor to a vegetable soup or a soup of rice and cabbage. It can also be mixed with the water for risotto with peas (see page 15).

CAVOLFIORE COLLA
BALSAMELLA
(*Cauliflower with Béchamel Sauce*)

All members of the cabbage family, be they white, red, yellow, or green, are children or stepchildren of Aeolus, god of the winds. Therefore people who cannot tolerate wind should have no difficulty remembering that these plants are called *crucifers*, since for such people these vegetables are truly a cross to bear. The real reason for the name, however, is that the flowers of these plants have four petals arranged in the shape of a cross.

Remove the leaves and the green stems from a large head of cauliflower, make a deep crosslike cut in the stalk, and cook in salted water. Then cut into small sections and season with butter, salt, and pepper. Place in an ovenproof dish, sprinkling with a little grated Parmesan cheese and covering with béchamel sauce. Cook until the surface is golden brown.

Serve hot as an *entremets*, or better yet accompanied by a stewed meat or boiled chicken.

SPARAGI (*Asparagus*)

To make asparagus look better, before cooking scrape the white part with a knife and cut off the end of the stem; then tie the stalks in bunches – not too large – with a string. To keep them green, drop them into salted water when it is boiling hard, and fan the fire so that the water boils up again immediately. When the spears start to bend, they are cooked just right; still you should check from time to time, testing them with your fingers to see if they give a little when you exert some pressure – it is better to undercook them a little than to overcook them. After you have strained the asparagus spears, drop them in cold water, and then strain them again immediately so that you can serve them warm, the way most people like them.

This vegetable, which is prized not only for its diuretic and digestive qualities, but also for the high price it commands, can be prepared in various ways once it is blanched. The simplest and best is the most common way, which is to season with the very finest olive oil and vinegar or lemon juice. Nevertheless, for variety, here are some other ways to prepare asparagus after it has been parboiled. Place the stalks whole in a pan and sauté lightly in butter. After seasoning with salt, pepper, and a tiny pinch of Parmesan cheese, remove the stalks from the pan and pour the browned butter over them. Or, separate the green part from the white part and, taking an ovenproof dish, arrange them like this: sprinkle the bottom of the dish with grated Parmesan cheese and arrange the asparagus spears next to one another, season with salt, pepper, grated Parmesan, and dabs of butter; make another layer of asparagus and season in the same way, continuing until you have used them all. Be spare with the other ingredients, however, so that the dish does not turn out excessively rich. Crisscross the layers of asparagus like a tight lattice, place under the lid of a

Dutch oven to melt the butter, and serve hot. If you have some brown stock, parboil the asparagus and finish cooking in the stock, adding a little butter and a light sprinkling of Parmesan cheese.

The bad smell that results from eating asparagus can be turned into the pleasant fragrance of violets by pouring a few drops of turpentine into the chamber pot.

Seafood

Of the common types of fish, the finest are: sturgeon, dentex, sea bass, weever, sole, turbot, John Dory, gilt-head sea bream, rock mullet, and fresh-water trout; these are excellent year round, but sole and turbot are especially good in the winter.

The seasons for the other best-known fish are: for hake, eel, and flying squid, year round, while eel is better in winter and flying squid in the summer.

For large gray salt-water mullet, July and August; for small mullet, October and November, and all winter. For gudgeon, whitebait, and cuttlefish, March, April, and May. For octopus, October. For sardines and anchovies, all winter, until April. For red mullet, September and October. For tuna, from March to October. For mackerel, springtime, especially May; this fish, on account of its tough and fibrous flesh, is usually used in stews – if you want to grill it, it is a good idea to put it on the fire on a large sheet of greased cooking paper and season it with oil, salt, pepper, and a few sprigs of rosemary.

Of the crustaceans, one of the most prized is lobster, which is good year round, but better in springtime, and of the shellfish, oysters, which are harvested from October to April in oyster beds.

When a fish is fresh, its eyes are bright and clear; if it is not fresh, the eyes are pale and cloudy. Another indication of freshness is the red color of the gills; but since these can be artificially colored with blood, touch them and then smell your finger; your nose will tell you whether it is fresh or not. Another characteristic of fresh fish is the firmness of the flesh, because if it is kept on ice too long it begins to decay and becomes soft to the touch.

Sailors say that crustaceans and sea urchins are meatier when gathered during a full moon.

CACCIUCCO
(Fish Stew)

Cacciucco! Let me say just a little bit about this word, which is understood perhaps only in Tuscany and on the shores of the Mediterranean, since on the shores of the Adriatic it is called 'brodetto' (literally, 'little broth'). In Florence, 'brodetto' means a soup with bread and broth, bound with beaten eggs and lemon juice. In Italy the confusion between these and other names from province to province is such that it is almost a second Tower of Babel.

After the unification of Italy, it seemed logical to me that we should think about unifying the spoken language, and yet few can be bothered with such an undertaking and many are outright hostile to it, perhaps because of false pride and the ingrained habit that Italians have of speaking their own regional dialect.

To return to cacciucco, let me say that, naturally enough, this is a dish prepared in seaside towns more than anywhere else, because it is there that you can find fresh fish of the kind needed to make it. Any fishmonger can tell you the varieties of fish that are best suited to a good cacciucco.

Good as it may be, however, it is still quite a heavy dish, so one needs to be careful not to gorge oneself on it.

For 700 grams (about 1½ pounds) of fish, finely chop an onion and sauté it with oil, parsley, and two whole cloves of garlic. The moment the onion starts to brown, add 300 grams (about 10½ ounces) of chopped fresh tomatoes or tomato paste, and season with salt and pepper. When the tomatoes are cooked, pour in one finger of strong vinegar or two fingers of weak vinegar, diluted in a large glass of water. Let boil for a few more minutes, then discard the garlic and strain the rest of the ingredients, pressing hard against the mesh. Put the strained sauce back on the fire along with whatever fish you may have on hand, including sole, red mullet, gurnard, dogfish, gudgeon, mantis shrimp, and other types of fish in season, leaving the small fish whole and cutting the big ones into large pieces. Taste for seasoning; but in any case it is not a bad idea to add a little olive oil, since the amount of soffritto was quite small. When the fish is cooked, the cacciucco is usually brought to the table on two separate platters: on one you place the fish, strained from the broth, and on the other you arrange enough finger-thick slices of bread to soak up all the broth. The bread slices should be warmed over the fire but not toasted.

SOGLIOLE IN GRATELLA
(Grilled Sole)

When sole (*Solea vulgaris*) are large, it is better to grill them and season with lard instead of olive oil; they take on a more pleasing flavor this way.

Clean the fish, scrape off the scales, rinse, and dry well. Then dab them lightly with cold virgin lard (making sure that it does not taste rancid); season with salt and pepper and coat with bread crumbs. Melt a little more lard in a frying pan and brush this on the fish; brush again with melted lard when you turn them on the grill.

When you prepare sole for frying, you can skin them on both sides or just on the dark side, then dredge in flour, keeping in beaten egg for several hours before tossing them in the pan.

A singular thing about this fish that merits mentioning is the fact that, like all well-constructed animals, it is born with one eye on its right side and the other on the left. But at a certain period in its life the eye that was on the white (or left) side migrates over to the right side and settles, like the other eye, on the dark side. Sole and turbot swim on their blind sides. Because of the quality and delicacy of its flesh, the French call sole the 'partridge of the sea.' It is a fish that is easy to digest, it resists decomposition better than many other fish, and it does not go out of season. It is found in abundance in the Adriatic, where it is caught at night with huge sack-like nets weighted down heavily at the mouth; when these nets scrape the bottom of the sea, they lift up the fish along with the sand and mud in which they lie.

Turbot, the flesh of which is not very different from that of sole, and is even more delicate, is called the 'pheasant of the sea.'

TRIGLIE COL PROSCIUTTO
(*Red Mullet with Prosciutto*)

The saying 'mute as a fish' is not always true, because red mullet, umber, and some other fish emit odd sounds caused by the vibration of special muscles; these vibrations are increased by the movement of the air in their swimming bladder.

The largest, most flavorful red mullet are rock mullet or striped surf mullet. However, this recipe can also be used for cooking medium-sized red mullet, which are called 'rossioli' or 'barboni' in the regions bordering the Adriatic. After gutting and rinsing the fish, dry them well with a kitchen towel, and then place them in a bowl and season with salt, pepper, oil, and lemon juice. Leave them like this for several hours, and when you are about to cook them, cut thin slices of untrimmed prosciutto. The slices should be as wide as and equal in number to the pieces of fish. Take a metal dish or pan and scatter a few whole sage leaves on the bottom. Coat the fish well in bread crumbs, and arrange them upright side by side with the slices of prosciutto between them, scattering more sage leaves on top.

Finally, pour the remaining liquid over the fish and bake with fire above and below. If you want this dish to turn out more refined, remove the spine from the raw mullet by cutting open the belly side, and then close the fish.

STORIONE (*Sturgeon*)

I hope my readers will allow me to give a little of the history of this very interesting fish.

The sturgeon belongs to the order of the *Ganoidei*, from the Latin *Ganus*, which means shiny, owing to the shine of its scales, and to the sub-order of the *Chondrostei*, since it has a cartilaginous skeleton. It constitutes the family of the *Acipenser*, which is defined by those two characteristic qualities, as well as by a skin made up of five longitudinal series of shiny scales. The mouth of this fish is located on the underside of the head; it has no teeth and is shaped like a protractile suction device, with nasal barbels or tentacles for searching in the mud for its food, which apparently consists of tiny creatures.

Sturgeon are highly prized for their flesh, as well as for their eggs, which are used for caviar, and for their enormous air bladder, which is used to make isinglass or fish glue. In the springtime, they swim upstream in rivers to deposit their eggs in calm waters along the banks.

Italy is home to several species of sturgeon, of which the most highly prized for its food is the *Acipenser sturio* (common sturgeon). It can be recognized by its sharp snout and thick lower lip split in the middle, as well as by its simple nasal tentacles, which are all the same size. It prefers the mouths of the Ticino and Po rivers, where not long ago one weighing 215 kilograms (about 475 pounds) was caught. But the sturgeon that grows largest is the *Acipenser buso*, which can reach up to two meters or more in length, with egg sacs one third the size of the entire fish. It is this fish in particular that provides caviar and gelatin. Caviar is made from the raw eggs of the sturgeon, which are carefully strained through a sieve to remove the filaments that envelop them; they are then salted and tightly packed. Isinglass is made on the beaches of the Caspian Sea and along the banks of the rivers that run into it, but more than anywhere else in Astrakhan. It is hardly surprising that there is such an extraordinary amount of it on the market (since isinglass has many uses), if one considers that sometimes in the Volga from fifteen to twenty thousand sturgeon are caught daily; for it is from there – that is, the southern regions of Russia – that we get caviar. It was announced not long ago that some fishermen on the Danube caught a sturgeon weighing 800 kilograms (about 1,950 pounds). The skeleton of this enormous fish, 3.3 meters (about 11 feet) long, is now on display at the Museum of Vienna.

The extinct species of sturgeon include the *Magadictis*, which reached a length of 10 to 20 meters (about 33 to 34 feet).

PASTICCIO DI MAGRO
(Seafood Pie)

I would be failing to give credit where it is due if I didn't tell you that I owe quite a few recipes in this book to the kindness of several ladies, who also favored me with this one. Although it looks like a true pasticcio, when I tried it, it came out worthy to be served at a dinner party, if prepared properly.

a fish weighing between 300 and 350 grams (between
    about 10½ and 12¼ ounces)
200 grams (about 7 ounces) of rice
150 grams (about 5¼ ounces) of fresh mushrooms
300 grams (about 10½ ounces) of green peas
50 grams (about 1⅔ ounces) of toasted pine nuts
butter, as needed
Parmesan cheese
6 artichokes
2 eggs

Cook the rice in 40 grams (about 1⅓ ounces) of butter
with a quarter of a chopped onion and salt it. When it
has cooked in the necessary amount of water, bind it
with the two eggs and 30 grams (about 1 ounce) of Parmesan cheese.

Make a soffritto of onion, butter, celery, carrot, and
parsley, and cook the sliced mushrooms, peas, and parboiled quartered artichokes in it. Finish cooking these
ingredients with a few tablespoons of hot water and season with salt, pepper, and 50 grams (about 1⅔ ounces) of
grated Parmesan cheese after you remove it from the fire.

Cook the fish, which can be mullet, weever, or some
other large fish, in a mixture of oil, garlic, parsley, and
tomato sauce or tomato paste; season with salt and pepper. Remove the fish from the fire, strain the sauce, and
stir in the pine nuts, which you have toasted and
crushed. Remove the head, spine, and bones from the
fish, cut it into small pieces, put it back in the broth,
and add all the other ingredients except the rice.

Now that all the ingredients for the filling are ready,

make the dough for the pie to contain it. Here are the proportions:

400 grams (about 14 ounces) of flour
80 grams (about 2⅔ ounces) of butter
2 eggs
2 tablespoons of white wine or Marsala
a pinch of salt

Roll out the dough and use it to line a mold greased with butter. Pour in first half of the rice, then all the filling, and finally the remaining rice over the filling; cover the top with more of the same dough. Bake in the oven, remove from the mold, and serve lukewarm or cold.

Made with the amounts indicated, this recipe serves twelve people.

ARINGA INGENTILITA
(*'Civilized' Herring*)

All you drinkers out there can put your forks down; this herring (*Clupea harengus*) is not for your jaded palates.

Ordinarily, people want the female herring because it is showier on account of the large amount of eggs; but the male, with its milky sperm sac, is more delicate and therefore preferable. Whether male or female, open the herring along the back, discard the head, and flatten it; then place it in scalded milk and let it sit for eight to ten hours. It would be well to change the milk once during this time. After drying it with a kitchen towel, cook on the grill like ordinary herring and season with oil and a very small amount of vinegar, or with oil and lemon juice if you prefer.

There is also another way to remove the salty flavor from herring. Place it on the fire in cold water, bring to a boil and simmer for three minutes, and then soak in cool water for a moment. Dry, discard the head, open along the back, and season as above.

Clupea harengus is the most common variety of the very important family of the *Clupeidae*, which also includes allice shad, pilchards, anchovies, sardines, and the *Alosa vulgaris*, or *Clupea comune*, which is called 'cheppia' ('shad') in Tuscany. In the spring, they swim upriver to deposit their eggs; at this time they are caught even in the Arno River in Florence.

Herring live in huge numbers at the bottom of the seas at the outer reaches of Europe, and are seen on the surface only at mating time – that is, during the months of April, May, and June. After they deposit their eggs they disappear into the depths of their usual abode. Sometimes the sea appears shimmering and translucent for several miles around because of the frenzy of the spawn and the scales that come loose during it. In England the herring run from July to September; the catch, done with round nets, is at times so abundant that on the shores of Yarmouth they have filled as many as five hundred thousand barrels with herrings.

BACCALÀ ALLA FIORENTINA
(*Salt Cod Florentine Style*)

'Baccalà' belong to the family of *Gadidae*, the most typical variety being cod. The most common species in our seas are the *Gadus minutus* and the *Merlucius esculentus* or hake, quite a bland fish but one that is easy to digest on account of its light flesh. It is good for convalescents, especially when poached and seasoned with oil and lemon juice.

The genus *Gadus morrhua* is the cod from the Arctic and Antarctic regions which, depending upon how it is prepared, is called either 'baccalà' (salt cod) or 'stocca-fisso' (stockfish). As everyone knows, an oil used for medicinal purposes is extracted from the liver of this fish. It is fished with a hook; a single man can catch up to 500 in one day. It is perhaps the most fecund of all fish – nine million eggs have been counted in a single individual.

There are two well-known types of cod on the market, Gaspé and Labrador. The former comes from the Gaspé Peninsula, that is the Banks of Newfoundland (where every year more than 100 million kilograms of cod are caught); it is dry, tough, and difficult to soften. The latter, which is caught along the coast of Labrador, is fat and tender, perhaps on account of a more copious food supply; it softens easily and is much better tasting.

Salt cod enjoys a good reputation in Florence, and deservedly so, because the Florentines know how to soften it well, cleaning it frequently with a little hard brush. Moreover, the cod consumed in Florence is usually the best Labrador cod, which is fatty by nature and relatively tender, considering the tough, fibrous flesh of this type of fish, which is not suited to weak stomachs. For this reason, I have never been able to digest it. On days of fasting, this salted fish competes on the market to great advantage with fresh fish, which is limited in quantity, high in price, and often not particularly fresh.

Cut the salt cod into pieces as wide as the palm of your hand and coat thoroughly with flour. Then put a large pan on the fire with a generous amount of oil and two or three whole garlic cloves, slightly crushed. When the garlic begins to brown, toss in the pieces of cod and brown on both sides, moving the fish around constantly to keep it from sticking. It is not necessary to add salt, or if you do, very little and only after tasting; but a pinch of pepper will not do any harm. At the end, pour in a few tablespoons of tomato sauce (see page 21), or tomato paste diluted in water. Boil a little longer and serve.

BACCALÀ FRITTO
(Fried Salt Cod)

The frying pan is an implement used for many lovely things in the kitchen; but, in my opinion, salt cod comes to a most deplorable end in it. This is because, since it has to be boiled first and then coated with batter, there is no seasoning that can give it a proper flavor. And yet some people, perhaps not knowing a better recipe, make the concoction that I am about to describe. To boil it, put it on the fire in cold water, and the moment it starts to boil, take it off the hearth, for it is already cooked. Without doing anything else, it can be eaten like this, seasoned with oil and vinegar.

But let's return to the concoction I mentioned. Feel free to try it, or to send both the recipe and whoever wrote it to the devil. After you have boiled the cod, marinate it whole in red wine for several hours; then dry it with a kitchen towel and cut it into small pieces, removing the spine and bones. Coat lightly with flour and dip in a simple batter made with water, flour, and a drop of oil, with no salt. Fry in oil and sprinkle with sugar after it has stopped sizzling. If eaten hot, the aroma of the wine is barely noticeable. If, however, you still find this to be an inferior dish, it is your fault for wanting to try it.

Roasted Meats

With the exception of birds and squabs, with which whole sage leaves go well, it is no longer customary to lard or baste spit-roasted meats, or to stud them with garlic, rosemary, or other aromatic herbs that tend to leave an aftertaste. If you have some good olive oil, baste them with that; otherwise, use lard or butter, depending on local preference.

People generally prefer roasted meats savory, so be generous with salt when you prepare milk-fed veal, lamb, kid, poultry, and pork. Be more sparing with meat from larger or older animals and with birds, because these meats are already quite flavorful in themselves. But always salt meat halfway or even two-thirds of the way through the cooking. People who salt any kind of meat before putting it on the spit are making a serious mistake, because the fire will dry it out and make it tough.

Pork and the meat of nursing animals such as veal, lamb, kid, and the like, should be cooked well in order to dry out their excessive moisture. Cook beef and mutton much less; being dry meats, you want them to remain juicy. Cook birds over a flame, but be careful not to overdo them, for they would lose a great deal of their fragrance. But take care that birds are not undercooked when you want to remove them from the fire; you can test for this by pricking them under the wing to check

71

whether any blood still runs out. You can tell whether chickens are done by pricking them in the same way.

Poultry will come out more tender and with a better color if you roast it wrapped in paper that has been buttered on the side touching the meat; to prevent the paper from burning, baste it frequently on the outside. Halfway through the cooking, remove the paper and finish cooking the chicken, turkey, or what have you, salting and basting it. If you use this method, it is also a good idea to put a little salt inside the bird before putting it on the spit, and to stud the breast of turkeys and guinea fowl with lardoons. I should point out here that squab and fattened capon, whether roasted or boiled, are better eaten cold than hot; they also have less of an aftertaste when eaten cold.

More than any other way of preparing meats, roasting preserves their nourishing properties, and makes them easier to digest.

ROAST BEEF

This English word has come into Italian as 'rosbiffe' and it means exactly what it says. A good roast beef is a very satisfying dish at a meal where the male gender predominates, since men are not satisfied with trifles the way women are. They want to sink their teeth into something solid and substantial.

The best cut for roast beef is the loin. In order to turn out tender, it should be from a young animal. It should weigh more than 1 kilogram (about 2 pounds) so that the fire will not dry it out, for the beauty and succulence of this dish depend on it being cooked just right, as is shown by a pink color on the inside and the copious juice that runs out when you slice it. Cook over a very hot fire from the start, so that the outer surface cooks quickly; baste with oil, which you will later drain from the dripping pan, and at the end pour a ladleful of broth over it; this, along with the fat that has dripped from the meat, will provide the sauce that you serve with the roast. At the halfway point, salt sparingly, because this type of meat is savory by itself, as I have already said. Always remember that salt, which is good in itself, is the worst enemy of good cooking when used to excess.

Put the meat on the spit half an hour before you serve the first course; this should be sufficient if the piece is not too large. To test for doneness, prick it at the thickest part with a thin larding needle, but do not make too many holes in it, or it will dry out. The juice that runs out should not be blood colored, nor too dark. Pan fry some raw, peeled potatoes in oil to serve as a side dish. If they are small, leave them whole; if large, cut into quarters.

Roast beef can also be made in the oven, but it doesn't come out as well as when cooked on a spit. If you make it in the oven, season with salt, oil, and a bit of butter, surround it with raw, peeled potatoes, and pour a glassful of water into the roasting pan.

If you do not like leftover roast beef cold, slice it and sauté in butter and brown stock or tomato sauce (see page 21).

POLLO AL DIAVOLO
(*Chicken Devil Style*)

It is called this because it is supposed to be seasoned with strong cayenne pepper and served with a very spicy sauce, so that whoever eats it feels his mouth on fire and is tempted to send both the chicken and whoever cooked it to the devil. I shall give a simpler, more civilized way to prepare it.

Take a cockerel or young chicken, remove the head, neck and feet, and, after cutting it open all the way down the front, flatten it out as much as you can. Wash and dry it well with a kitchen towel, then place it on the grill. When it begins to brown, turn it over, brush with melted butter or olive oil and season with salt and pepper. When the other side begins to brown, turn the chicken over again and repeat the procedure. Continue to baste and season as necessary until done.

Cayenne pepper is sold as a red powder, which comes from England in little glass bottles.

GALLINA DI FARAONE
(*Guinea Hen*)

This fowl, originally from Numidia and therefore erroneously called Indian hen, was a symbol of brotherly love in ancient times. When Meleager, king of Calydon, died, his sisters mourned him so deeply that Diana transformed them into guinea hens. The *Numida meleagris*, which is the domestic guinea hen, is still half wild, unfriendly and restless; it resembles the partridge both in its habits and in the flavor of its delicate flesh. Poor creatures, they are so pretty! They are usually killed by cutting their throats, although some people prefer to drown them, keeping them under water by force – a cruel practice, like so many others invented by the gluttony of man. The meat of this bird needs to ripen for quite some time; during the winter, it will keep ungutted for at least five or six days.

The best way to cook guinea hens is to roast them on a spit. Place a ball of butter rolled in salt inside the bird, stud the breast with lardoons, and wrap in a sheet of paper greased with cold butter and sprinkled with salt. Remove the paper when the bird is two-thirds cooked; then brown it over the flame until done, basting with oil and salting it again.

A young turkey can be cooked in the same way.

Pastries, Cakes, and Sweets

STRUDEL

Do not be alarmed if this dessert seems to you to be a strange concoction, or if it looks like some ugly creature such as a giant leech or a shapeless snake after you cook it; you will like the way it tastes.

500 grams (about 1 pound) of reinette apples, or tender,
*   good quality apples*
250 grams (about 8⅘ ounces) of flour
100 grams (about 3½ ounces) butter
85 grams (about 3 ounces) of dried currants
85 grams (about 3 ounces) of powdered sugar
grated rind of one lemon
2 or 3 pinches of ground cinnamon

Make a fairly firm dough with the flour, warm milk, a piece of butter about the size of a walnut, an egg, and a pinch of salt. Allow the dough to rest a little before using it, then roll it out in a sheet as thin as the one for taglierini noodles. Cover the sheet of dough with a layer of apples (peeled, cored and thinly sliced), leaving the edges free. Scatter the currants, lemon peel, cinnamon, sugar, and finally the 100 grams (about 3½ ounces) of melted butter over the layer of apple slices. Reserve a little of the butter to use later. This done, roll the sheet of dough up so that if forms a nice cylinder of dough and filling, which you will fit into a round copper pan greased with butter. Pour the leftover melted butter all over the outside of the roll, and place it in the oven. Remember that dried currants or sultanas are different from raisins, which are small and dark. Currants and sultanas are twice as large, light brown in color, and seedless. Scrape the lemon peel with a piece of glass.

BISCOTTI DELLA SALUTE
(Health Cookies)

Cheer up, for if you eat these cookies you will never die, or you will live as long as Methuselah. I eat them often, in fact, and when some indiscreet person sees me more sprightly than is becoming to my venerable age and asks me how old I am, I answer that I am as old as Methuselah, son of Enoch.

350 grams (about 12⅓ ounces) of flour
100 grams (about 3½ ounces) of brown sugar
50 grams (about 1⅔ ounces) of butter
10 grams (about ⅓ of an ounce) of cream of tartar
5 grams (about ⅕ of an ounce) of baking soda
2 eggs
a dash of vanilla sugar
milk, as needed

Mix the flour with the sugar and make a mound with a hole in the middle where you will drop the rest of the ingredients, adding a little milk to obtain a rather soft dough. Shape the dough in a slightly flattened cylinder about half a meter long. Grease a baking pan with butter, and divide the loaf into two parts so that it will fit in the pan. Make sure that the two parts are well separated, because they swell a great deal when baked. Bake in an oven or a Dutch oven. The next day, cut the loaves into cookies, which should number about thirty or so, and toast in the oven.

PASTA MARGHERITA
(*Sponge Cake*)

One day my dear departed friend Antonio Mattei from the town of Prato (of whom I will have occasion to speak again) tasted this pastry at my house and asked for the recipe. Being an industrious man, it didn't take him long to refine and perfect the recipe and begin to sell it in his shop. Later he told me that the success of this sweet was so great that hardly a dinner was given in Prato without it being ordered. People wishing to make their way in the world are quick to grasp any opportunity to seduce Lady Fortune, who – though capricious in how she dispenses her favors – is never a friend to the idle and lazy.

120 grams (about 4¼ ounces) of potato flour
120 grams (about 4¼ ounces) of powdered sugar
4 eggs
the juice of one lemon

First, thoroughly beat the egg yolks and the sugar. Add the flour and lemon juice and work for more than half an hour. Lastly, beat the egg whites and fold them into the rest of the ingredients; but do so gently, so that they don't go flat. Pour the mixture into a smooth round mold or an appropriately sized baking pan, greased with butter and dusted with confectioners' sugar mixed with flour, and place immediately in the oven. Let cool, then remove from the mold and sprinkle with vanilla confectioners' sugar.

STIACCIATA UNTA
(*Greased Flat Cake*)

The portions for this cake and for the Mantuan cake were recommended to me by that good man, the late Antonio Mattei of Prato, whom I've already mentioned earlier. I say 'good' because he was a genius in his art and was an honest, very industrious man. But this dear friend of mine, who always reminded me of Boccaccio's character Cisti the baker, died in the year 1885, leaving me deeply grieved. Letters and science aren't always necessary to win public esteem; even a very humble art, accompanied by a kind heart and practiced with skill and decorum, can make us worthy of the respect and love of our fellow men.

> *Beneath rough manners and humble exteriors*
> *often lie noble hearts and pure souls;*
> *we should be wary of men who are too genteel,*
> *for they are like marble: shiny, smooth, and hard.*

But let's get to the point:

700 grams (about 1½ pounds) of leaven dough
120 grams (about 4¼ ounces) of lard

100 grams (about 3½ ounces) of sugar
60 grams (about 2 ounces) of cracklings
4 egg yolks
a pinch of salt
orange or lemon zest

Knead the dough gently so that it doesn't lose its elasticity. If you make it in the evening and set it aside in a warm place, it will rise by itself; if you make it in the morning, it will need three hours in an earthenware warming oven.

If you want to make it without cracklings, add two more egg yolks and 30 more grams of lard.

Half of this recipe will serve five or six people.

PANETTONE MARIETTA
(*Marietta's Panettone*)

My Marietta is a good cook, and such a good-hearted, honest woman that she deserves to have this cake named after her, especially since she taught me how to make it.

300 grams (about 10½ ounces) of extra-fine flour
100 grams (about 3½ ounces) of butter
80 grams (about 2⅔ ounces) of sugar
80 grams (about 2⅔ ounces) of sultanas
one whole egg and two yolks
a pinch of salt
10 grams (about ⅓ of an ounce) of cream of tartar
a teaspoon or 5 scant grams (about ⅕ of an ounce) of
  baking soda

20 grams (about ⅔ of an ounce) of candied fruit, in tiny pieces
lemon zest
about 2 deciliters (about ⅘ of a cup) of milk

In wintertime, soften the butter in *bain-marie* and then blend it with the eggs. Add the flour and milk a little at a time, then the rest of the ingredients except the sultanas, cream of tartar, and baking soda, which you should keep for the last. But before adding them, work the mixture for at least half an hour and dilute it with the milk until it's the right consistency – not too liquid, and not too firm. Pour into a mold twice as large as the amount of batter, deeper than it is wide, so that when it rises it doesn't overflow, and it will come out in the shape of a round loaf. Grease the sides of the mold with butter, dust with powdered sugar mixed with flour, and bake in the oven. If it turns out right, it should rise a great deal, and have a puffed-up, dome-shaped top with cracks in it. This panettone is worth trying, because it's much better than the Milanese-style panettone that's sold commercially, and isn't much trouble to make.

OFFELLE DI MARMELLATA
(*Scalloped Sweet Pastries with Fruit Filling*)

The word 'offella,' in this context, comes from the dialect of Romagna, and, if I'm not mistaken, it is used in the Lombard dialect as well. It probably derives from the ancient word *offa*, which means a flat cake or bread made with spelt and various other ingredients.

Dar l'offa al cerbero, 'to give Cerberus a sop,' is a rather timely expression, since there are so many people these days who seek out public office so that they can gorge themselves on public funds. But we'd better get back to offelle.

500 grams (about 1 pound) of red apples
125 grams (about 4½ ounces) of powdered sugar
30 grams (about 1 ounce) of candied fruit
two teaspoons cinnamon powder

Cut the apples into four sections, peel, and core. Slice the sections as thin as possible and put in a saucepan on the fire with two glasses of water; break apart with a wooden spoon. Since these apples have firm flesh, they need to be cooked in water; if they start to dry out while you're cooking them, just add some more water. Wait until the apples have become mushy before adding the sugar, and then taste to see if they're sweet enough, since fruit in general can be more or less acid, depending upon how ripe it is. Lastly, add the candied fruit, chopped into small pieces, and the cinnamon.

Use shortcrust pastry dough. Spread it out with a rolling pin until it's the thickness of a coin. Then cut it with a round pastry cutter with a scalloped edge. With one disk of dough underneath and one on top (the latter rolled with a ridged rolling pin), put the cooked apple mixture in the middle and moisten the edges so that the two disks of dough stick together. Gild with egg yolk, and bake. Afterward, sprinkle with confectioners' sugar.

CAVALLUCCI DI SIENA
(*Sienese 'Little Horses'*)

The specialty sweets of Siena are panforte, ricciarelli, cavallucci, and cupate. Cavallucci are little pastries shaped liked mostaccioli. You can see that they have nothing to do with horses, and I don't think that they even know why they're called that in Siena, a city, as the saying goes, *where three things abound: towers, bells, and quintains*.

In this recipe I want to give you a close, but not exact imitation of Sienese cavallucci – we've got the flavor just about right, but the consistency leaves something to be desired, which is only natural. When something is made in large quantities and with methods that are kept secret from the uninitiated, any imitation is bound to falter.

300 grams (about 10½ ounces) of flour
300 grams (about 10½ ounces) of blond sugar
100 grams (about 3½ ounces) of shelled walnuts
50 grams (about 1⅔ ounces) of candied orange
15 grams (about ½ of an ounce) of aniseed
5 grams (about ⅕ of an ounce) of spices and cinnamon
    powder

Chop the walnuts into pieces about the size of beans. Dice the candied orange. Put the sugar on the fire with a third of its weight in water, and when it has reached the point where it threads from the spoon, add all of the

83

other ingredients and blend. Pour the hot mixture over the flour on a pastry board – but to do this, you'll see that you'll need more flour to give the dough the right consistency. Then form the cavallucci, of which, with these amounts, you should get more than 40. Since the dough is quite sticky on account of the sugar, dust the cookies all over with flour. Place in a baking pan and bake them plain, at moderate heat. Be very careful when you cook the sugar, because it will turn dark if it cooks too much. Pick up a drop between your thumb and index finger, and if it starts to form a thread, it's cooked enough for this recipe.

FAVE ALLA ROMANA O DEI MORTI
(*Roman-Style Sweet Fava Beans, or Dead Men's Beans*)

These sweets are usually made for the Day of the Dead, and they take the place of the *baggiana*, the garden-variety fava bean, which is typically cooked in water with a ham bone for this occasion. This custom must have originated in antiquity, since the fava bean was used as an offering to the Fates, Pluto, and Persephone, and was famous for the superstitious ceremonies in which it was used. The ancient Egyptians abstained from eating the fava; they didn't plant it, nor did they touch it with their hands. Their priests wouldn't even dare to look upon it, deeming it a vile thing. Fava beans, especially black favas, were used as a funeral offering because it was believed that they contained the souls of the dead, and were similar to the gates of Hell.

During the feasts of the *Lemures*, people would spit out black fava beans while beating a copper pot, to chase out of their homes the spirits of their ancestors, the souls of the departed, and the infernal deities.

Festus claimed that there was a funereal sign on the flowers of this legume; and they say that the custom of offering fava beans to the dead was one of the reasons that Pythagoras ordered his students to abstain from eating them; another reason was to prevent them from getting involved in government affairs, since fava beans were used for balloting in elections.

There are several ways to make sweet favas. Here are three different recipes: the first two are family style; the third is more refined.

First recipe

200 grams (about 7 ounces) of flour
100 grams (about 3½ ounces) of sugar
100 grams (about 3½ ounces) of sweet almonds
30 grams (about 1 ounce) of butter
1 egg
a dash of lemon zest, or cinnamon, or orange-flower water

Second recipe

200 grams (about 7 ounces) of sweet almonds
100 grams (about 3½ ounces) of flour
100 grams (about 3½ ounces) of sugar
30 grams (about 1 ounce) of butter
1 egg
flavoring, as above

Third recipe

200 grams (about 7 ounces) of sweet almonds
200 grams (about 7 ounces) of confectioners' sugar
2 egg whites
lemon zest or other flavoring

For the first two recipes, blanch the almonds and crush them with the sugar until they are half as big as a grain of rice. Put them in the middle of the flour along with the other ingredients, and make a soft dough using as much rosolio or brandy as necessary. Then make the dough into small pastries shaped like large fava beans; you should get 60 or 70 for each recipe. Arrange in a baking pan greased with lard or butter and dusted with flour; gild with egg yolk. Bake in the oven or Dutch oven. Remember that since they are so small, they bake very quickly. For the third recipe, dry the almonds in the sun or on the fire and crush them very fine in a mortar, adding the egg whites a little at a time. Lastly, add the sugar and, using your hand, mix together. Pour the dough onto a pastry board over a thin layer of flour. Shape into a long roll and cut it into forty or more pieces. Shape like fava beans and bake as in the preceding recipes.

BRIGIDINI (*Brigettine Cookies*)

This is a sweet, or rather an amusing treat local to Tuscany, where it can be found at all the country fairs and festivals. You can see it being cooked in the open air in waffle irons.

2 eggs
120 grams (about 4¼ ounces) of sugar
10 grams (about ⅓ of an ounce) of aniseed
a pinch of salt
flour, as much as needed

Prepare a rather firm dough, kneading it on a pastry board, and shape into nut-sized nuggets which you will place in a waffle iron at an appropriate distance from one another. Turn the iron this way and that over a wood fire, and remove when brown.

Cakes and Spoon Desserts

Not to boast unduly, but to amuse the reader and satisfy the wish of an anonymous admirer, I here publish the following letter, which reached me on July 14, 1906 from Portoferraio, as I was correcting the galley proofs of *Science in the Kitchen and the Art of Eating Well*.

Esteemed Mr. Artusi,

A poet gave me as a gift your lovely book *La scienza in cucina*, adding a few lines of verse, which I transcribe below. Perhaps they may be of use if you print another edition, which I hope you will do in the very near future.

Della salute è questo il breviario,
L'apoteosi è qui della papilla:
L'uom mercé sua può viver centenario
Centellando la vita a stilla a stilla.
Il solo gaudio uman (gli altri son giuochi)
Dio lo commmise alla virtù de' cuochi;
Onde sè stesso ogni infelice accusi
Che non ha in casa il libro dell'Artusi;
E dieci volte un asino si chiami
Se a mente non ne sa tutti i dettami.

Un ammiratore

(This little manual is about health and well-being,
a true apotheosis of the taste buds,

Thanks to which a man can live a hundred years
Sipping life to the fullest drop by drop.
The only joy people have (the rest are a mockery)
God entrusted to the talent of cooks;
So that you have only yourself to blame
If you do not have *Artusi* on your shelves;
And you should call yourself an ass ten times over
If you have not learnt his precepts by heart.

An Admirer)

TORTA DI PATATE (*Potato Cake*)

Although we are dealing with the humble potato here, do not scoff at this cake, which is worth making. And if your dinner guests cannot detect the plebeian origins of this cake when they taste it, conceal it from them, for they would only scoff.

Many people eat more with their imagination than with their palate. Accordingly, never mention, at least until your guests have finished eating and digesting what you have served them, foods that are considered inferior for the sole reason that they are inexpensive or because they evoke associations that some people might find distasteful. Yet these very foods, when used well and handled correctly, make for good, tasty dishes. Let me now tell you a story on the subject. Once I found myself invited to dine with some close friends. Our host, to impress us, made a little joke about the roast he was serving, for he remarked: 'None of you can complain about the way I am treating you today: we have three different varieties of roast meat: milk-fed veal, chicken and rabbit.' At the word 'rabbit' some of the guests turned up their noses, others seemed dumbfounded, and someone, a close friend of the family, said: 'What on earth did you decide to feed us! At least you could have kept quiet. You've made me lose my appetite.'

At another dinner party, when by chance the conversation turned to 'porchetta' – a suckling pig of 50 to 60 kilograms (about 110 to 132 pounds), stuffed with spices and roasted whole on a spit – one lady cried out, 'If I were offered such filth to eat, I could not possibly do it!' The host, stung by the aspersion she had cast on a dish that was held in high esteem in his part of the country, invited the woman a second time to his house, when he prepared a lovely cut of lean porchetta. She not only ate it but, believing it was milk-fed veal, thought that the roast tasted delicious. I could tell you many similar tales; but I cannot pass over in silence the case of a certain gentleman who, finding a particular pie quite delicious, ate enough for two days. But when he discovered that the pie was made of pumpkin, not only did he never eat it again, but he would also give it such a sinister look you would have thought the pie had seriously offended him.

Now here is the recipe for potato cake.

700 grams (about 1½ pounds) of big starchy potatoes
150 grams (about 5¼ ounces) of sugar
70 grams (about 2⅓ ounces) of sweet almonds and 3 bitter
* almonds*
5 eggs
30 grams (about 1 ounce) of butter

a pinch of salt
a dash of lemon peel

Boil the potatoes (or better yet, steam them). Peel and purée, passing them through a strainer while they are still hot. Blanch the almonds and crush in a mortar together with the sugar, until you have a very fine paste. Then add this mixture and all the other ingredients to the potatoes, stirring everything with a wooden spoon for a whole hour, breaking in the eggs one at a time, and then pouring in the melted butter. Place the mixture in a baking pan greased with butter or lard and dusted with bread crumbs. Bake in the oven and serve cold.

* * *

If I were not afraid of annoying the reader, here would be an opportune moment for another digression on German cooking.

As long as I live, I will never forget the array of foods spread out on a big hotel's buffet at the spa town of Levico. From the fried foods and the boiled dishes, all the way to the roasts, all swam in gallons of the same sauce, that always tasted and smelled alike, with what delight to the stomach you can just imagine. And just to add to the torture, very often these dishes were served accompanied by a timbale of angel hair pasta – angel hair, you understand, the thinnest pasta on the planet! – which when prepared in this way must suffer a doubly long cooking time: a bloody mess.

How utterly at odds with our Italian way of doing things! My cook has standing orders to remove angel hair from the water when it has barely begun to boil, and I am already waiting at the table.

Italian cuisine can rival the French, and in some respects actually surpasses it. However, due to the hordes of invading foreigners who bring us, apparently, about 300 million lire annually and, according to rough calculations, an extra 200 million lire in gold during the Jubilee Year of 1900, our cuisine is slowly beginning to lose its special character in the swirl of wandering nations. These unfortunate changes to our diet have already begun to appear, particularly in the large cities and in those areas heavily frequented by foreigners. I recently became convinced of this on a trip to Pompeii, where my traveling companion and I were preceded into a restaurant by a group of German tourists, both male and female, and were served in the same fashion as they were. When the proprietor later came up and courteously asked how we liked our dinners, I took the liberty of commenting on the nauseating slop of seasonings we had just been served. He replied, 'Our cooking has to please these foreigners, since this is how we make our living.' Perhaps this is the same reason Bolognese cuisine has begun to change, as I have heard, and no longer deserves the reputation it once had.

TORTA TEDESCA (*German Cake*)

Our grandfathers used to tell how toward the end of the 1700s, when the Germans invaded our country, there was still something uncivilized in their customs. For example, they used to provoke everyone's horror by preparing broth with tallow candles that they plunged in a pot of boiling water, then squeezing out the wicks. But when, unfortunately, they descended on us again in 1849, they appeared much more civilized. Then tallow could only be seen on Croat militiamen's long mustachios, which were smeared with it so that they could be twisted and their tips rolled to finger-length points that stood up straight and stiff. Nonetheless, from what visitors to that country tell me, tallow has kept a place in German cooking, a cuisine which Italians find in the worst possible taste and positively nauseating, as it uses all manner of fat and makes slop-like soups utterly lacking in flavor.

On the other hand, however, everybody agrees Germans can make delicious desserts. You personally, dear reader, may judge for yourself the truth of this assertion, both from the cake I am about to describe, as well as from some of the other desserts born in Germany that I have offered you in this treatise of mine.

250 grams (about 8⅘ ounces) of sugar
125 grams (about 4½ ounces) of flour
125 grams (about 4½ ounces) of sweet almonds
100 grams (about 3½ ounces) of butter
15 grams (about ½ an ounce) of cream of tartar
5 grams (about ⅕ of an ounce) of baking soda
8 egg yolks
5 egg whites
a dash of vanilla

Blanch the almonds, dry them well in the sun or on the fire, and then crush in a mortar until very fine, adding one of the egg whites. Beat the butter alone with a wooden spoon; in wintertime soften it a little first in *bain-marie*. Add the egg yolks one at a time, then the sugar and blend everything well for at least half an hour. Then add the almonds to the mixture and stir some more. Then fold in the four egg whites (beaten until stiff) and the flour, which you will sift on top of the mixture, stirring gently. Add the cream of tartar and the baking soda at the last, as they will make the cake lighter and softer. Bake in a baking pan well greased with cold butter and lightly dusted with confectioners' sugar and flour. The pan should not be too full.

The only way to blend the almonds satisfactorily into the mixture is to pour a portion of the mixture into the mortar over the almonds and then crush with the pestle.

Now that you have made the cloak, it is time to fashion the hood, which is a light icing that you spread on top of the cake. Here is what you will need:

100 grams (about 3½ ounces) of butter
100 grams (about 3½ ounces) of confectioners' sugar
30 grams (about 1 ounce) of finely ground coffee

Bring the ground coffee to a boil in very little water until you get just two or three tablespoons of clear but very strong coffee. Beat the butter for half an hour (in wintertime softening it first in *bain-marie*), turning the spoon always in the same direction. Add the sugar and stir some more. Finally mix in the coffee a little at a time, in half teaspoons. Stop when you can clearly taste the coffee flavor. Pour this mixture over the cake after it has cooled, and spread it out evenly with a table knife. To make it uniform and smooth, pass a hot spatula just above the icing.

Normally, this very delicately flavored icing should have the color of *café-au-lait*. If you like, instead of coffee you can use melted chocolate.

DOLCE ROMA (*Rome Cake*)

A gentleman whom I do not have the pleasure of knowing personally kindly sent me this recipe from Rome, and I am very grateful to him for it for two reasons: first because this is a dessert of very elegant appearance and flavor, and second because he described it in such a way that I had no difficulty at all testing the recipe. One thing was missing, however, and that was a name for it, since it had none. Thus, considering the nobility of its provenance, I felt it my duty to associate this dessert with Turin Cake and Florence Cake, naming it after the city that one day will be as famous in the world as it once was in Antiquity.

Select quality apples, not too ripe and of average size. Weigh out 600 grams (about 1⅓ of a pound), which should amount to no more than five or six apples. Remove the cores with a hollow tin corer, and peel. Then cook in 2 deciliters (about ⅘ of a cup) of white wine and 130 grams (about 4½ ounces) of sugar, taking care not to break the apples when you turn them as they cook, and not to overcook them. When done, remove them from the pot and arrange them upright in a platter nice enough to use for serving but ovenproof as well. Pour over them a custard made of the following ingredients:

4 deciliters (about 1⅔ cups) of milk
3 egg yolks
70 grams (about 2⅓ ounces) of sugar
20 grams (about ⅔ of an ounce) of flour
a dash of vanilla sugar

Now whisk the three remaining egg whites. When they are quite stiff, add 20 grams (about ⅔ of an ounce) of confectioners' sugar and cover the custard with it. Then place the cake in a Dutch oven or on the stove under the lid of the Dutch oven, with fire above and a low fire below, to brown the surface of the cake. Before serving, dab the cake with the thick syrup left over from cooking the apples, using a baker's brush.

This recipe serves seven to eight people.

BUDINO DI FARINA DI RISO
(Rice Flour Pudding)

This very simple dessert possesses, in my opinion, a very delicate flavor, and although almost everyone has tried it at one time or another, it would not hurt to learn the exact ingredients and quantities, which I think should not be increased or decreased.

1 liter (about 1 quart) of milk
200 grams (about 7 ounces) of rice flour

120 grams (about 4¼ ounces) of sugar
20 grams (about ⅔ of an ounce) of butter
6 eggs
a pinch of salt
a dash of vanilla

First, dissolve the rice flour in a fourth of the cold milk; then put on the fire. When the mixture starts to boil, add a little more warm milk, and finally pour in the rest of the milk when it is at a full boil. This is to prevent lumps from forming. When cooked, add the sugar, the butter and the salt. Remove from the fire and wait until lukewarm before folding in the eggs and the vanilla. Now bake the pudding and serve hot.

This recipe, which in all likelihood is not very old, makes me think that dishes, too, are subject to fashions, and that tastes change in accordance with progress and civilization. Now we prize light cuisine and dishes that are pleasing to the eye, and perhaps there will come a time when many of the dishes I consider good will be replaced by others even better. The sweet, heavy wines of an earlier era have given way to the dry, full-bodied vintages of today; the baked goose stuffed with garlic and quinces, regarded as a delicacy in 1300, has been replaced by turkey fattened domestically and stuffed with truffles, and by capon in galantine. In the olden days, on great occasions they used to serve boiled or roasted peacock, still arrayed in all its plumage, which was removed before preparing the bird and replaced after the bird was cooked. Then the peacock was served surrounded by aspics of various shapes, colored with mineral powders injurious to the health, and flavored with such spices as cumin and scented red clay ('bucchero') – about which I will tell you shortly.

In Florence, sweet pastries and baked goods remained rather primitive and simple until the late 16th century, when a company of Lombards arrived and set about baking pies, little cakes, puffy turnovers and other pastries made with eggs, butter, milk, sugar, and honey. But before that, ancient records mention only the donkey-meat pies Malatesta gave as gifts to his friends during the siege of Florence, when shortages of every kind of food, particularly meats, were acute.

As for bucchero, there was a time when Spain was the fashion trendsetter, just as France is today, and all nations tried to imitate its style of cuisine and flavoring. Thus, at the end of the 17th century and the beginning of the 18th, Spanish-style fragrances and aromas became extremely popular. Above all fragrances, however, bucchero turned everyone's head, and so widespread was its use that ultimately spice merchants and stewards started putting it in tablets and foodstuffs, just as is done with vanilla today. From what fabulous substance was bucchero extracted and what did it taste like? You will be stunned when you hear. Now judge for yourself the extravagant folly of tastes and people! Bucchero consisted of powdered shards of pottery, and its odor resembled that which the earth scorched by the summer sun exhales when rains fall. It is the same smell of earth that is given off by those dark-red, thin and brittle vases called buccheri, which perhaps gave their name to a dark red color, although the most prized were a glossy black. Vases of this material were first imported into Europe from South America by the Portuguese, who used them as drinking vessels and to boil perfumes and colognes; later, the fragments were used in the manner I just described.

In Homer's *Odyssey* (XVIII, 43–49), Antinous says:

> Gentlemen, quiet! One more thing:
> here are goat stomachs ready on the fire
> to stuff with blood and fat, good supper pudding.
> The man who wins this gallant bout
> may step up here and take the one he likes.
> And let him feast with us from this day on:
> no other beggar will be admitted here
> when we are at our wine.
>
> (trans. Robert Fitzgerald)

In volume 6 of the *Florentine Observer*, we find the following description of a unique dinner that deserves to be quoted in part:

'Among the most sumptuous dishes there was also peacock, stewed with its feathers, and colored gelatin, molded in various shapes. A man in Siena, who was preparing a supper for a courtier of Pope Pius II named Goro (around 1450), was given such bad advice regarding these two items, that he became the butt of jokes all over Siena. Particularly amusing was the fact that, unable to find peacocks, he substituted wild geese, removing their feet and bills.

'When the beakless peacocks were served, the

command was given to begin carving them up. But the person in charge did not know how to do it, and though he struggled with the birds for a long time he only succeeded in filling with feathers the banquet hall and the table, as well as the eyes, mouth, nose and ears of Messer Goro and everyone else . . .

'When that accursed bird was removed from the table, many other roasts prepared with a great deal of cumin were served. Nonetheless, everything still might have been forgiven, had not the master of the house and his misguided advisers decided to further honor their guests with a platter of aspic which they ordered custom made for the occasion. Inside the aspic they had the cooks place, as is sometimes done in Florence and elsewhere, replicas of the papal coat of arms, as well as of Messer Goro's crest and additional heraldic figures. So they used orpiment, white lead, cinnabar, verdigris and other absurdities to make these fantastic patterns inside the aspic. Then they set it before Messer Goro as a festive dish and something new and wonderful. He and all his company ate it happily enough, as a way to get rid of all the bitter flavors left in their mouths by the excessive cumin and the other strange dishes.

'And it was a miracle that some of the guests did not die during the night, and first among them Messer Goro, who had a horrible headache and stomachache, and very likely vomited a small bouquet of wild feathers. After these infernal and deadly courses, a great many sweets were served, and the dinner came to an end.'

PUDDING CESARINO

I consider this Cesarino a good boy, and I shall sell his pudding to you under the same strange name it bore when I bought it from a young and rather lovely woman, upright and religious, the sort who, without intending to, can by her flirtatious nature compromise anyone in her immediate vicinity.

200 grams (about 7 ounces) of extra fine crustless bread
250 grams (about 8⅘ ounces) of sugar
approximately 100 grams (about 3½ ounces) of additional
    sugar, for use in the mold
125 grams (about 4½ ounces) of Malaga raisins
125 grams (about 4½ ounces) of sultanas
½ liter (about ½ a quart) of milk
3 tablespoons in total of Marsala wine and rum
5 eggs

Cut the crustless bread into thin slices, and soak it in the milk. Meanwhile, clean the sultanas, remove the seeds from the Malaga raisins and prepare the mold for cooking. Use a copper mold intended for puddings. Put about 100 grams (about 3½ ounces) of the sugar into a saucepan and, once it has turned nut brown, pour it into the mold, coating it thoroughly. After the mold has cooled, grease the sugar glaze with cold butter.

Combine the milk-soaked bread with the other 250 grams (about 8⅘ ounces) of sugar, the egg yolks and the liquors. Blend everything thoroughly. Finally, add the raisins and fold in the egg whites, beaten until stiff. Place the mixture in the mold prepared as described above, then put the mold in *bain-marie*, and cook for three whole hours; but heat from above only for the last hour. Serve hot as a flambé, sprinkling rum generously over the pudding and setting it ablaze with a table-spoonful of lit spirits.

These amounts should be enough for ten to twelve people.

MIGLIACCIO DI ROMAGNA
(*Romagna Blood Pudding*)

Se il maiale volasse
Non ci saria danar che lo pagasse.

(If pigs had wings to fly on,
you couldn't afford to buy one.)

This is what someone once said; and someone else replied: 'A pig, with all the cuts of meat it provides, and all the various manipulations these cuts can be subjected to, lets you taste as many flavors as there are days in a year.' I let the reader decide which of these two silly sayings comes closer to the mark. As for myself, I will be happy to evoke the so-called 'pig's wedding,' for even this filthy animal can be amusing, but, just like the miser, only on the day of his death.

In Romagna, well-to-do families and peasants slaughter pigs at home, which is an occasion to make merry and for the children to romp. This is also a great opportunity to remember friends, relatives and other people towards whom you may have some obligation by making a gift of three or four loin chops to one, a slab of liver to another, while sending to yet a third a good plate of blood pudding. The families receiving these things will of course do the same in return. 'One gives bread in exchange for flour,' one might say. But regardless, these are customs that help maintain goodwill and friendships among families.

Coming at last to the point, after this preamble, here is the recipe for Romagna blood pudding. On account of its nobility this blood pudding would not even deign to recognize as kin the sweet-flour blood pudding you can find on any street corner in Florence:

7 deciliters (2⅖ cups) of milk
330 grams (about 11⅔ ounces) of pig's blood
200 grams (about 7 ounces) of concentrated must, or
    refined honey
100 grams (about 3½ ounces) of shelled sweet almonds
100 grams (about 3½ ounces) of sugar
80 grams (about 2⅔ ounces) of very fine bread crumbs
50 grams (about 1⅔ ounces) of minced candied fruit
50 grams (about 1⅔ ounces) of butter
2 teaspoons allspice
100 grams (about 3½ ounces) of chocolate
1 teaspoon nutmeg
a strip of lemon peel

Crush the almonds in a mortar together with the candied fruit, which you have first diced, moistening the mixture now and then with a few teaspoons of milk. Then pass through a sieve. Boil the milk with the lemon peel for ten minutes, then remove the lemon peel, add the grated chocolate and stir until melted. Remove the milk from the fire and let it cool a little. Then pour into the same bowl the blood, which you have already passed through a sieve, and all the other ingredients, adding the bread crumbs last, so that if you have too much you can leave some of it aside.

Cook the mixture in *bain-marie*, stirring often so as not let it stick to the bowl. You will know that the mixture has achieved the right consistency and is done when the mixing spoon remains upright, if you stand it in the center of the mixture. If this does not happen eventually, add the rest of the bread crumbs, if you have not already used all of them. Pour the mixture into a baking pan lined with crazy dough and when it has cooled completely, cut it into almond shaped pieces. Cook the dough as little as possible, so that it is easier to slice, and do not let the pudding dry out over the fire, but rather remove it from the hearth as soon as the broom-twig with which you are pricking it to test for doneness comes out clean.

If you are using honey instead of the concentrated must, taste it before adding the sugar to avoid making it too sweet, and keep in mind that one of the beauties of this dish lies in a creamy consistency.

My fear of not being understood by everyone often leads me to provide too many details, which I would gladly spare the reader. Still, some people never seem to be satisfied. For instance, a cook from a town in Romagna wrote to me: 'I prepared the blood pudding described in your highly esteemed cookbook for my employers. It was very well liked, except that I didn't quite understand how to pass the almonds and the candied fruit through the sieve. Would you be good enough to tell me how to do this?'

Delighted by the question, I answered her: 'I am not sure if you know that you can find sieves made especially for this purpose. One type is strong and widely spaced, and is made with horsehair. Another is made of very fine wire. With these, a good mortar and *elbow-grease*, you can purée even the most difficult things.'

Ice Creams

I read in an Italian newspaper that the art of making ice cream belongs preeminently to Italy, that the origin of ice cream is ancient, and that the first ice creams in Paris were served to Catherine de' Medici in 1533. This article added that the Florentine pastry makers, chefs, and icers of the royal palace would not share knowledge of their art. As a result the secret recipe for making ice cream remained within the confines of the Louvre, and Parisians had to wait another century to taste ice cream.

All my research to verify this story has been in vain. One thing that is sure on the subject of ice cream is this: the use of snow and stored ice to produce iced drinks is of oriental origin and goes all the way back to remote antiquity. Ice creams came into fashion in France around 1660, when a certain Procopio Coltelli from Palermo opened a shop in Paris under his own name: *Café Procope*. The establishment was across from the *Comédie Française*, which was then the meeting place of all the Parisian *beaux esprits*. The immediate success of this place, which was the first to serve ice cream in the shape of an egg in stemmed cups, drove the vendors of lemonade and other drinks to imitate it. Among these should be remembered Tortoni, whose delicious ice creams were so in vogue that his café acquired a European reputation, and made him his fortune.

According to Atheneus and Seneca, the ancients built ice boxes to store snow and ice using a technique not so different from ours today, namely: digging deep into the earth and, after compacting the ice and snow, covering them with oak branches and straw. But the ancients did not yet know the properties of salt, which when added to ice accelerates the freezing process, making it much easier to make sherbet with liqueurs of every kind.

You will almost surely please all your dinner guests, especially in the summer, if at the end of the meal you offer them sherbet or ice cream. These desserts, in addition to satisfying one's palate, also aid digestion by recalling heat to the stomach. And today, thanks to the American ice cream makers, which have triple action and need no spatula, making ice cream has become so much easier and faster that it would be a shame not to enjoy much more frequently the sensual pleasure of this delicious food.

To save money you can re-use the salt by drying it out on the fire, thus evaporating the water that had resulted from the freezing process.

PONCE ALLA ROMANA
(*Roman Punch*)

This recipe serves six people.

Lately, this kind of ice cream has become popular at fancy dinner parties. It is usually served before the roasted meat course, because it aids digestion and prepares the stomach to receive the remaining courses.

450 grams (about 1 pound) of sugar
5 deciliters (about 2 cups) of water
2 oranges
2 lemons
2 egg whites
1 small glass of rum
a dash of vanilla

Boil 250 grams (about 8⅘ ounces) of the sugar in 4 deciliters (about 1⅔ cups) of water with a little lemon and orange peel. Remove from the fire and squeeze the juice of the oranges and lemons into the syrup. Strain the mixture through a cloth, and pour it into the ice cream maker to freeze.

Put the remaining 200 grams (about 7 ounces) of sugar in the remaining 1 deciliter (about ⅖ of a cup) of water, add the vanilla, and boil until a drop does not run when poured onto a plate or makes a thread when tested between two fingers. By now you will have beaten the egg whites quite stiff, and you are ready to pour the syrup over them while it is still very hot. Then beat well to obtain a smooth consistency. After this mixture has cooled, combine it with the ice cream and blend well. Add the rum just before sending to the table in stemmed glasses.

MACEDONIA (Mixed Fruit Ice Cream)

And now we bid welcome to Madam Macedonia, to whom I would rather give the simpler name of 'Mixed Fruit Ice Cream,' a dessert that will be especially welcome in the scorching months of July and August.

For this dessert, if you do not have an ice cream mold, you can use a tin-plated metal container (shaped like a mess tin or a small saucepan) with a lid that can be hermetically sealed.

Take many varieties of fruit in season, ripe and of good quality, for example: red currants, strawberries, raspberries, cherries, plums, apricots, a peach and a pear. Starting with the cherries, peel all the fruit and chop to the size of pumpkin seeds, discarding the cores and stones. Use only a very small amount of red currants because their seeds are too big and too hard. Some fragrant melon would make a nice addition.

Weigh the fruit once you have prepared it in this manner; let's say you have 500 grams (about 1 pound) of fruit, then sprinkle 100 grams (about 3½ ounces) of confectioners' sugar on top, and add the juice of 1 garden lemon. Blend well and let sit for half an hour.

Use a piece of paper to line the bottom of the metal container, then pour in the fruit, packing it well. Cover the container and place it in a tub filled with ice and salt. Leave it to freeze for several hours. If it will not unmold easily, wet the sides of the container with warm water. It will make an attractive display as a frozen, marbled block of ice cream.

These amounts serve four to five people.

GELATO DI LATTE DI MANDORLE
(*Almond Milk Ice Cream*)

I describe the following dish especially for you, ladies of delicate, refined taste, for I am sure that you will find it delightful; and since I often think of you when I create these dishes, which, I hope, take into account and satisfy your taste, I must take advantage of this opportunity to say that I hope you long preserve the enviable qualities of blooming health and beauty.

200 grams (about 7 ounces) of sugar
150 grams (about 5¼ ounces) of sweet almonds, and 4 or
    5 bitter almonds
8 deciliters (about 3⅓ cups) of water
2 deciliters (about ⅘ of a cup) of heavy cream
a dash of orange-flower water or coriander seeds

Boil the sugar in the water for ten minutes together with the coriander seeds, if you are using the coriander or comfits for flavor. Blanch the almonds and crush them very fine in a mortar along with a few tablespoons of the syrup, then stir them into the syrup. Strain the mixture through a loosely woven cloth, squeezing well to extract as much of the flavor as possible; crush the almonds in the mortar with some syrup a few more times if necessary. Add the cream to the extracted liquid and then freeze in the ice cream maker. Once it has hardened, serve it in stemmed glasses.

This recipe serves nine to ten people.

GREAT  FOOD

A TASTE OF THE SUN

Elizabeth David

LEGENDARY COOK AND WRITER Elizabeth David
changed the way Britain ate, introducing a postwar nation
to the sun-drenched delights of the Mediterranean, and
bringing new flavours and aromas such as garlic,
wine and olive oil into its kitchens.

This mouthwatering selection of her writings and
recipes embraces the richness of French and Italian cuisine,
from earthy cassoulets to the simplest spaghetti, as well as
evoking the smell of buttered toast, the colours of foreign
markets and the pleasures of picnics. Rich with anecdote,
David's writing is defined by a passion for good, authentic,
well-balanced food that still inspires chefs today.

*'Above all, Elizabeth David's books
make you want to cook'*
TERENCE CONRAN

······· GREAT   FOOD ·······

A MIDDLE EASTERN FEAST
Claudia Roden

AWARD-WINNING FOOD WRITER Claudia Roden
revolutionized Western attitudes to the cuisines of the
Middle East with her bestselling *Book of Middle Eastern
Food*. Introducing millions to enticing new scents and
flavours, her intensely personal, passionate writings
conveyed an age-old tradition of family eating and shared
memory. This selection includes recipes for tagines from
Morocco, rice from Iran, peasant soup from ancient
Egypt and kofta from Armenia, as well as discussions of
spices, market bargaining, childhood memories of Cairo
and the etiquette of tea drinking; evoking not only a
cuisine but an entire way of life.

*'Roden's great gift is to conjure up not just a cuisine
but the culture from which it springs'*
NIGELLA LAWSON

GREAT   FOOD

RECIPES AND LESSONS FROM A DELICIOUS COOKING REVOLUTION

Alice Waters

A CHAMPION OF ORGANIC, locally produced and seasonal food and founder of acclaimed Californian restaurant Chez Panisse, Alice Waters has recently been awarded the *Légion d'honneur* in France for her contributions to food culture. In this book, she explores the simplest of dishes in the most delicious of ways, with fresh, sustainable ingredients a must, even encouraging cooks to plant their own garden.

From orange and olive salad to lemon curd and ginger snaps, Waters constantly emphasizes the joys and ease of cooking with local, fresh food, whether in soups, salads or sensual, classic desserts.

'Waters is a legend'
JAY RAYNER

GREAT 🐧 FOOD

THROUGHOUT the history of civilization, food has been livelihood, status symbol, entertainment – and passion. The twenty fine food writers here, reflecting on different cuisines from across the centuries and around the globe, have influenced each other and continue to influence us today, opening the door to the wonders of every kitchen.